Manhood

A JOURNEY FROM CHILDHOOD INTO THE FIERCE ORDER OF VIRILITY

Michel Leiris

TRANSLATED FROM THE FRENCH BY
RICHARD HOWARD

North Point Press

SAN FRANCISCO 1984

TO

Georges Bataille

WHO IS AT THE ORIGIN OF THIS BOOK

Contents

Translator's Note, 1983

I should like to welcome MANHOOD back into print by an observation on its place; first of all, on its place in the canon of its author's work. Shapely as it is—indeed, carved rather than molten as most confessional works are likely to be (Retz, Rousseau, Renard)—the function of this book is liminary: it is the prologue to a vast, indeed to an interminable enterprise of that self-determination which is one of the two principal strains (in every sense of that word) in French literature.* The four volumes to which it offers such a serviceable threshold, volumes which continue what Susan Sontag, in her splendid essay greeting the book's translation twenty years ago, called Leiris's life-project, are named *Biffures* (erasures), *Fourbis* (leavings), *Fibrilles* (tendrils), *Frêle Bruit* (faint noise); all these words suggest the murmurous tentative venture that will conclude only with its author's own life, though they give no notion of the genuinely shocking nature of the erotic pursuits therein vivisected. *La Règle du jeu* (the rule of the game), as the entire work is called, is a limit-case, and if it can still shock and even offend us after the productions and exposures of the last twenty years (as it *does* shock its translator), then I venture to say it is doomed to retain its dire status forever. The finishing touch applied to this writer's work will be to burn it.

Yet MANHOOD stands by itself—it is one of the central works of what we may call modernity, and it addresses with an admirable (or perhaps with an alarming) intensity the process by which the pronoun *I* becomes—on the other side of "writing"—the pronoun *he*. That crucial recognition which we associate with Rim-

*Not of all literature in French, of course. I mean, by "French literature," that interconnecting structure of texts that appear to answer, and to ask, the same questions about the nature and disposition of the self and the City, from Joinville to Genet.

baud, the favorite expression of our alienation epitomized in the famous sentence *Je est un autre*, is in this book explored and, I might say, implored.

And it is precisely because of the availability of this recognition, the pathos of this imploration, that the little book takes its place within that other strain of French literature as well. I mean that not only does it seek out the limits, the limitations of the punished ego, but it thereby joins that ego to others, makes possible the acknowledgment of others we call society. This is the alternative emphasis, then, in French literature, and whether it is the self in solitude or the social self that is anatomized, we can see the governing impulses to be if not the same at least analogical. Pascal and Montaigne, Gide and Jouhandeau, Baudelaire and Balzac, Valéry and Sartre—these pairs, these duets are not arbitrary, they are exercises in nuance, they posit the self and the social, the reft or sundered ego and the possibility of cartilage, of connective tissue.

What is so particular about Leiris—Leiris the author, not the subject, the hero, the victim of MANHOOD—is that he has managed to institute these generally warring energies, these *frères ennemis*, psyche and culture, in a subtle structure of motives and acknowledgments—almost always acknowledgments of failure, of *fallings from us, vanishings*; the merest accounting of his body ("my hands are thin, rather hairy, the veins distinct . . .") takes Leiris into a fetishistic realm of self-loathing ("my two middle fingers, curving inward towards the tips, must denote something rather weak or evasive in my character")—which does a kind of fastidious justice to both. That is the exceptional quality of this self-strafing book, the saving grace that confers, by *literary authority*, its exemplary status on MANHOOD. The heroic enterprise is suggested, for example, by this passage near the book's close, one of the great enlightening flashes of the literature of abjection:

In November 1929, after various disappointments and disasters dating back to the spring before . . . I appeared at a friend's house around five in the morning and asked to borrow his razor with the—more or less sham—intention of castrating myself, a request my friend evaded by informing me that all he had was an electric razor. I realized that disease played a part in every one of these manifestations, and I decided to undergo psychoanalytic treatment. . . .

That conclusion is the beginning of a great adventure, one of the most honorable in French literature today, a literature that finds its generating *frappe* or mold in two sentences, this by Pascal: "I am very much afraid that this nature is itself no more than a first custom, as custom is a second nature," and this by Montaigne: "the laws of conscience, which we say are born of nature, are born of custom." Michel Leiris; or, Civilization and Its Discontents.

R.H.

Manhood

PROLOGUE

I HAVE just reached the age of thirty-four, life's mid-point. Physically I am of average height, on the short side. I have my auburn hair cut short to keep it from curling, and also to prevent the spread of an incipient baldness. As far as I can judge, the characteristic features of my physiognomy are: a straight nape, falling vertically from the back of my head like a wall or a cliff, a typical characteristic (according to the astrologists) of persons born under the sign of the Bull; a broad, rather bulging forehead with exaggeratedly knotty and projecting temporal veins. This expanse of forehead corresponds (the astrologers say) to the sign of the Ram; and indeed I was born on April twentieth, hence under the jurisdiction of these two signs: the Ram and the Bull. My eyes are brown, the edges of the lids habitually inflamed; my complexion is high; I am disconcerted by an irritating tendency to blush, and by a shiny skin. My hands are thin, rather hairy, the veins distinct; my two middle fingers, curving inward toward the tips, must denote something rather weak or evasive in my character.

My head is rather large for my body; my legs are a little short for the length of my torso, my shoulders too narrow in relation to my hips. I walk with the upper part of my body bent forward; I have a tendency, when sitting, to hunch my back; my chest is not very broad and I am not at all muscular. I like to dress with the greatest possible elegance; yet due to the defects I have just described in my physique and to my financial means, which, without my being able to call them poor, are rather limited, I usually consider myself profoundly inelegant; I loathe unexpectedly catching sight of myself in a mirror, for unless I have prepared myself for the confrontation, I seem humiliatingly ugly to myself each time.

Some of my gestures have been—or are—habitual: to sniff the back of my hand; to gnaw my thumbs almost until they bleed; to cock my head; to draw in my lips and nostrils with a look of resolution; to strike my forehead suddenly with my palm—like someone who has just had an idea—and keep it pressed there a few seconds (earlier, on such occasions, I fingered my occiput); to cover my eyes with my hand when I must answer yes or no about something that embarrasses me or reach a decision; to scratch my anal region when I am alone; etc. . . . I have abandoned these gestures one by one, at least for the most part. Perhaps, though, I have only replaced them by new ones which I have not yet identified. However accustomed I am to observing myself, however obsessive my predilection for this grim kind of scrutiny, there are doubtless things that escape me, and most likely the most apparent among them, since perspective is everything and a self-portrait, painted from my own observation, is often likely to leave in obscurity certain details which for other people would be the most flagrant.

My chief activity is literature, a term greatly disparaged today. I do not hesitate to use it, however, for it is a question of fact: one is a literary man as one is a botanist, a philosopher, an astronomer, a physicist, a doctor. There is no point in inventing other terms, other excuses to justify one's predilection for writing: anyone who likes to think with a pen in his hand is a writer. The few books I have published have won me no fame. I do not complain of this, any more than I brag of it, for I feel the same distaste for the "popular author" genre as for that of the "neglected poet."

Without being a traveler in any strict sense of the word, I have seen a certain number of countries: as a young man, Switzerland, Belgium, Holland, England; later, the Rhineland, Egypt, Greece, Italy, and Spain; quite recently, equatorial Africa. Yet I speak no foreign language fluently and this fact, along with many others, gives me a sense of inadequacy and isolation.

Although obliged to work (at a job that is not disagreeable to me, since my profession as an ethnographer is quite in accord with my tastes) I live in a certain comfort; I enjoy good health; I am relatively free, and from many points of view I must include myself with those who are conventionally called "happy in life." Yet there are few events in my existence that I recall with satisfaction; I suffer more and more acutely from the sensation of struggling in a trap and—without any literary exaggeration—it seems to me that I am being *corroded*.

Sexually I am not, I believe, abnormal—simply a man of rather cold temperament—but I have long tended to regard myself as virtually impotent. It has been some time, in any case, since I have ceased to consider the sexual act as a simple matter, but rather as a relatively exceptional event, necessitating certain inner accommodations that are either particularly tragic or particularly exalted, but very different, in either case, from what I must regard as my usual disposition.

From a less immediately erotic point of view, I have always suffered disgust for pregnant women, fear of childbirth, and frank repugnance toward newborn babies. Such emotions have, I believe, been familiar since my earliest childhood, and I suspect that such fairy-tale expressions as "they lived happily ever after and had many children" provoked an early incredulity.

My sister gave birth to a daughter when I was about nine; I was literally nauseated by my first glimpse of the child—the pointed skull, the diapers smeared with excrement, and the umbilical cord that made me exclaim: "She's throwing up out of her stomach!" Above all I could not bear being the youngest no longer, the one the family called the "little latecomer." I realized that I had ceased to represent the last generation; it was the revelation of *aging*; I felt great sadness and discomfort—and anguish which has subsequently grown only more intense.

As an adult, I have never been able to endure the idea of having a child, of bringing into the world a being who by definition has not asked for life and must endure death, after having, perhaps, procreated in its turn. It would be impossible for me to perform the sexual act if I felt it to be anything but sterile and alien to the human instinct of reproduction. This leads me to believe that love and death—to procreate and to perish, which come to the same thing—are so close to one another that any notion of carnal pleasure affects me only when it is accompanied by superstitious terror, as if the gestures of love, even as they work my life to its most intense pitch, can only bring me pain.

Although our union has been occasionally stormy because of my unstable character, my heartlessness, and particularly because of my huge capacity for boredom, from which everything else proceeds, I love the woman who shares my life and I am beginning to believe that I shall end my days with her, insofar as a man may make such an assertion without exposing himself to fate's bloody denial. Like many men, I have made my descent into Hell, and like some, I have more or less returned from it. On the far side of that abyss lies my early youth toward which, in recent years, I turn as toward the only happy period of my life, though already containing the elements of its own disintegration and all the features which, gradually deepening into wrinkles and lines, give my portrait its likeness.

Before attempting to trace some of the lineaments which withstand that degradation of the absolute, that gradual degeneration which for me expresses most of the passage from youth to maturity, I should like to set down here, in a few lines, what vestiges I can gather of the *metaphysic of my childhood*.

OLD AGE AND DEATH

IT IS impossible for me to discover when it was that I learned about death and by what means it ultimately assumed a reality in my mind, no longer meaning "to go to heaven." My mother sometimes took me to visit the graves of her family in Père Lachaise, where I saw displayed under a glass globe the Masonic insignia of my grandfather, a high official of the Third Republic, a disciple of Auguste Comte and a Venerable of the "Rose of Perfect Silence" Lodge. Finding the globe broken each time and the insignia desecrated by marauders, my mother at last renounced this exhibition of relics and was content to decorate the grave with flowers, everlastings, and slender wreaths of beads. These visits to the cemetery that was so far from the bourgeois—almost provincial—neighborhood where we lived certainly gave me a foretaste of something, though it was not yet really death.

I entertained a few disquieting notions about death, more exactly about *corpses* (one, in particular, that derived from an illustration in a magazine where, if I am not mistaken, a man was shown being struck by lightning, and in his eyes was the image of the tree under which he had been struck). I also had—or had a little later—certain notions of *suicide*, having got hold of an illustrated daily showing the suicide of a rajah and his wives on a huge pyre, an incident which must have occurred on some Malayan island or peninsula. The rajah was a rather young man, slender and yellow, wearing a black mustache and a plumed turban; his wives having been killed by his hand or put to death by his orders, he was shown stabbing himself in his turn; thrusting a long kris with a serpentine blade into his breast, he was silhouetted, already staggering, against the fire in the background.

I did not understand just what suicide was, and above all to what degree the will was involved in such an act; I wondered, for instance, if the wives the rajah had killed or ordered to be killed were suicides—whether their deaths had been voluntary or coerced. The only thing I perceived clearly was the word "suicide" itself, whose sonority I associated with the idea of fire and the serpentine shape of the kris, and this association was so deeply rooted in my mind that even today I cannot write "suicide" without again seeing the rajah in his setting of flames; there is the "s" whose shape as well as sound reminds me not only of the torsion of the body about to fall, but of the sinuosity of the blade; the "ui," which echoes strangely and insinuates itself, somehow, like the tongues of the fire or the zigzags of a lightning flash; the "cide," which concludes the word with an acid taste, implying something sharp and incisive.*

I note, then, that however vague my notion of death (it was scarcely more than a simple allegory for me: a skeleton armed with a scythe), I had at least some inkling of what a *violent* death might be: to be struck by lightning, or to commit suicide. People who died in their beds were members of my family, who by definition "went to heaven" and were promised eternal happiness. The rest were peculiar, almost monstrous, even damned. For me death was neither the sudden accident nor the tragic consumption by fire, and it was certainly not the loss of existence. It was the passage to the repose of the cemetery—to the double life of Paradise and the grave which pious hands kept bright with flowers.

If everything, consequently, remains vague as to the way in which I gradually grew aware of what death really is, I find one very clear material image which greatly contributed to my notion of the succession of life's stages, of the passage of time, of the transition to adulthood, then to decrepitude—in a word, of aging. This was a group of drawings which as a very young child I saw on the back cover of an album printed in Épinal, and which was called *The Colors of Life*. I am not sure I remember exactly what the colors were, nor to what specific phases of life they were supposed to correspond, but this is how they come to mind now.

The square at the top left corner was colored an indeterminate olive or mauve. On one side were newborn babies in cabbages, on the other, a baby in diapers, rubbing his eyes with his fists, supported under his arms by a circular, wheeled brace like our modern "walkers" and called "chariots" at the time.

I was very anxious to know whether I had outgrown this age and color. I often questioned my brothers about it. To tease me they said, of course, that I had not, and I was hideously mortified each time. I did not aspire to the higher stages; actually they melted into the night of time, and it never occurred to me that

* In French, *acide* rhymes with *suicide.—Translator's note.*

any one of them (except, perhaps, the age of marriage) might represent an apogee. I was simply anxious to grow out of the first muddy square and into the next, which was colored

pink, for adolescence, and which showed, beside a little boy leaning on a windowsill and blowing soap bubbles, a group of girls and boys playing together. My ambition was confined to this, and all the other squares—except perhaps the last—remained quite abstract.

Then came, among others:

blue, with lovers in the moonlight;

green, showing a touching maternal scene;

then the colors of maturity, the only ones, with the first two colors of childhood, that I remember with sufficient exactitude:

chestnut brown, corresponding to two drunk tramps of about forty, exchanging blows whose violence was expressed by many stars of various sizes;

red, showing a bearded man wearing a skull cap, sitting in a huge armchair, his slippered feet stretched out in front of a fire, recalling—as he smoked a good pipe—his memories of glory and valor, military scenes illustrated with bullet trajectories and exploding grenades—in the smoke from the glowing fire at which he was warming himself;

yellow (I'm not certain it was yellow, but for me the image meant: jaundice), showing a man of no particular age, almost sexless, bald, crooked, eccentric, wearing a nightcap and a dressing gown, and enjoying himself over a cup of tea;

gray, showing a family scene of the most classically optimistic kind: parents and grandparents handing around a tiny baby;

black, finally, where the essential element was a lugubrious, skeletal character, sitting in a kind of cellar where he was "grinding out darkness," it seemed to me, with the help of a machine with a crank like a coffee mill; he was wearing a top hat and black suit which made him look like an undertaker; his eyes and nose were running, and he was holding a guttering candle, the wax dripping onto the candlestick.

Each of these images must have had a title corresponding to its color. They must also have been more numerous, and certainly most of the ordinary occupations corresponding to the various ages of life were represented. However, I remember none of them aside from those I have just described; perhaps, then, they had not impressed me as much as I should like to think today.

Actually, the only one that remains really meaningful for me is the first, for it marvelously expresses that chaos which is the first stage of life, that irreplaceable state when, as in legendary days, all things are still undifferentiated, when the rupture between microcosm and macrocosm has not yet occurred and the self is steeped in a kind of fluid universe, as at the heart of the absolute.

I have now passed through a certain number of these colors, including, long before forty, that of the "chestnut brown." Yellow—or liver disease—lies ahead, and scarcely more than a year ago I tried to escape black by suicide. But that is how things happen, how things are done and undone; I am still caught in these Colors of Life, and I have less and less hope of escaping their order (at least by my own will), framed in the wooden oblong like a bad daguerreotype, spotted here and there with iridescent mould like the rainbow tints of decomposition on the faces of the drowned.

SUPERNATURE

ONE of the greatest enigmas of my earliest years, aside from the riddle of birth, was the means by which the Christmas toys got down the chimney. I evolved a Byzantine rationale to account for how the larger toys could logically get down the chimney if Father Christmas dropped them from above. Apropos of a large model sailboat (which, as I learned later, was a present from one of my older brother's friends) I solved the problem by accepting the following hypothesis: since God is omnipotent, he creates the toys just where I find them, without their having to pass through the chimney. My amazement at the sight of the enor-

mous boat at the bottom of the narrow shaft was something like
that which the sight of a ship inside a narrow-necked bottle in
a nearby shopwindow caused me each time I passed it.

When I learned that children were created in the womb, and
when the mystery of Christmas was explained to me, I felt I had
acceded to a kind of majority; this was connected in my mind
with the concept of the Age of Reason, a period when—in prin-
ciple—the first degree of initiation is passed. Once I knew what
pregnancy was, the problem of childbirth became analogous to
that of how the toys got down the chimney: How did the baby
get out?

INFINITY

I OWE my first actual contact with the notion of infinity to a tin
of Dutch cocoa, the raw material of my breakfasts. One side of
the tin was decorated with an image of a farm girl in a lace cap,
holding in her left hand an identical tin, decorated with the
same image of the smiling, pink girl. I still get dizzy imagining
this infinite series of an identical image endlessly reproducing
the same Dutch girl who, theoretically shrinking without ever
disappearing, mockingly stared at me, brandishing her own effigy
painted on a cocoa tin identical to the one on which she herself
was painted.

I suspect that mingled with this first notion of infinity, acquired around the age of ten (?), was a somewhat sinister element: the hallucinatory and actually ineffable character of the
Dutch girl, infinitely repeated the way licentious poses can be
indefinitely multiplied by means of the reflections in a cleverly
manipulated boudoir mirror.

THE SOUL

A LITTLE later, when I was at school and already possessed some
idea of cosmography, I had the following image of the soul,
which I knew was only a pure fantasy but which was nonetheless

indissolubly linked for me to my image: one of those dry pieces of dough with a long needle through it, called "bird cakes," that I thrust between bars of the cage to feed the baby birds.

It is more than likely that this image came from the following experiment, described in an elementary geography textbook; I transcribe it here as I recall it, not troubling to check whether or not I am reproducing it exactly: a mass of oil being suspended within a liquid is pierced by a needle which is then made to rotate rapidly; swept on by the needle, the mass of oil, at first virtually spherical, submits to the action of centrifugal force and flattens somewhat, by which phenomenon we can conceive what happens in the case of the earth, which is not strictly spherical but slightly distorted in a manner analogous to that in which the mass of oil is flattened by the effect of its rotation on the axis of the needle. If the needle's rotation becomes quite rapid, the distortion increases; then a part of the mass is detached and forms a ring, as occurred in the case of the planet Saturn.

This identification of the soul with the bird cake—or even with a Candlemas cake, pierced in the same way through the middle—was based, I believe, on my belief in the material existence of my soul, which I could not imagine save as a solid body, though of indeterminate substance and irregular shape—a solid lodged perhaps in some fold of my brain but essentially aerial or weightless, related to birds (bird cake) or bats (the flat Candlemas cake, thin as the wings of the bat, and flipped up out of the pan, reproducing—near the dimness of the stove, the heavy smoke, and the soot—a clumsy flight comparable to the mysterious swoops of these nocturnal animals).

SUBJECT AND OBJECT

DURING my early years, I was not interested in the outer world, save as a function of my most immediate needs, or of my fears. The universe was almost entirely circumscribed in myself, contained between those two poles of my concern which were, on the one hand, my "moon" (as I had been taught to call my posterior in baby talk), and on the other my "little machine" (the name my mother gave to my genitals). Nature was nothing but a source of suspicion, either because I had been warned about the snakes that swarm in the Forêt de Fontainebleau (and above all, apparently, in places where there are bushes—to such a degree that I imagined that each little mauve heather-flower contained a viper's egg), or because my mother had warned me, when I played in the Bois de Boulogne, never to listen to what "nasty men" might tell me in order to kidnap me; such people, she said, hung around the fort and the Auteuil racetrack, vague creatures who I sensed were none other than satyrs. They must have played the same role for me as gypsies in the minds of country children: elves, fauns, demons of nature, the disturbing side of the anthills and charcoal-burners' huts. Later, I conceived of them as cannibals, because of the drawing in *Pêle-Mêle* showing savages—purplish-gray with gangrene—eating an explorer. They were also the people in the agony columns, which I was told "were not for me," an expression later applied to pornographic publications, another face of this same strange world.

At the age of six or seven, I was walking one day with my mother, my brothers, and my sister in a woods on the outskirts of Paris near the region where my family used to spend the summer in those days. We sat in a clearing to eat our picnic lunch, and quite unexpectedly this place became the site of my first erection. The event which caused my excitement was the sight of a group of children—boys and girls about my own age—climbing trees barefoot. I was overcome, by pity I thought, an emotion I had been taught to feel toward "poor children." At the time, I established no direct relation between the modification in my penis and the spectacle before me; I simply remarked on the strange coincidence. Much later, it seemed to me that the strange sensation I experienced then came from imagining what must have been both a pleasant and a painful feeling for the children in question, the feeling caused by the contact of the soles of their feet and their bare toes with the rough bark. Perhaps their ragged, poverty-stricken aspect played an immediate part in my disturbance, as well as the touch of vertigo engendered by the apprehension of their fall.

Whatever the case, this sudden erection, mysterious as to its cause since I discerned no link between the scene which had provoked it and the phenomenon itself, corresponded to a kind of eruption of nature into my body, a sudden manifestation of the outer world, since without yet being capable of finding the solution to the riddle, I at least noted a coincidence implying a parallel between two series of facts: what was happening in my body, and external events, of which I had hitherto taken no account since they occurred in another realm.

I ATTACH no excessive importance to these recollections from various stages of my childhood, but it is convenient for me to collect them here at this moment, for they are the frame—or the fragments of the frame—within which everything else has been set. Much more decisive, it seems to me, were certain precise facts, some whose influence I have never doubted (those relating to the theater and particularly to the opera), others whose more secret significance has been revealed to me only fortuitously, in the light of a painting by Cranach representing two particularly alluring female figures: Lucrece and Judith.

The sight of these two figures—to which I have attached, perhaps arbitrarily, an allegorical significance—utterly confounded me several years ago, toward the end of a psychological treatment which my inner anguish had obliged me to undertake in spite of my repugnance for anything claiming to cure ills other than those of the body. Hence it occurred to me to write these pages, primarily a simple confession based on Cranach's painting, with the goal of liquidating, by formulating them, certain obsessions whose weight oppressed me; in the second place, an epitome of recollections, a panoramic view of a whole aspect of my life.

I could compare what such a gallery of recollections repre-

sents for me now to what the rosary that hung at the head of my
bed meant before I was seven: the world divided into tens (with
a bigger bead separating each group and a cross at the end)
capable of being held in my hand; or else all of the vegetable
realm contained (in the form of sweet peas, nasturtiums, snap-
dragons) in the tiny garden I used to cultivate in the country; or
else the strange sign that I wonderingly discovered when I cut
the fern stems, and which—a real Solomon's-seal—seemed to me
to condense my entire universe.

If this were a play, one of those dramas I have always loved so
much, I think the subject could be summarized like this: how the
hero—that is, Holofernes—leaves for better or worse (and rather
for worse than better) the miraculous chaos of childhood for the
fierce order of virility.

I

Tragic Themes

FAUST

Mephistopheles, can't you see
a beautiful pale girl, standing alone
and far away? Slowly she drags herself along,
as if her feet were chained. It seems to me,
I must confess, she's very like my Gretchen.

MEPHISTOPHELES

Let that alone! It's no good! It's a magic image,
lifeless, a phantom. It's bad luck to meet it.
That rigid stare would "thick men's blood with cold"
and almost turn you into stone.
Haven't you heard about Medusa?

FAUST

Truly, they are the eyes of a dead girl,
unclosed by loving hands. That's the sweet breast
that Gretchen gave me, the body I enjoyed.

MEPHISTOPHELES

It's sorcery, deluded simpleton!
Every man sees in her his own beloved.

FAUST

What joy and what torture!
I cannot leave this vision.
How strangely that one scarlet thread,
no thicker than the blade of a knife,
decorates her lovely neck!

MEPHISTOPHELES

That's right! I see it too.
She can carry her head away, neatly under her arm,
for Perseus sliced it off.

(GOETHE, *Faust*, Part I, MacIntyre translation)

A LARGE part of my childhood was under the sign of plays, operas, or lyric dramas that I was taken to by my parents, both passionately fond of the theater, particularly when it was combined with music. They frequently had a box at the opera lent them by my father's chief client, a wealthy woman whose funds he managed for her. From this box—the second from

the stage on the right side of the hall—I watched, from my tenth
year on (leaning far over the edge, for even from the first row of
the box, it was difficult to see more than the left half of the stage)
many productions in the repertory: *Romeo and Juliet, Faust,
Rigoletto, Aïda, Lohengrin, Die Meistersinger von Nürnberg,
Parsifal, Hamlet, Salome;* and perhaps it is from the impression
these performances made upon me that I still have the habit of
proceeding by allusions, by metaphors, or of behaving as if I
were in a theater.

Without calculating all that might have been either sincere or
feigned about such an emotion, I can say that I wept at the death
of the lovers of Verona, went into ecstasies over the ballerinas in
tights, the gilded cardboard cups, the spinning lights and other
splendors of the Walpurgisnacht (a name which, because of its
second and third syllables, made me think of "orgy"); I trembled
when Rigoletto killed his daughter by mistake, shared the
agonies of Radames and Aïda smothering in their subterranean
prison, abandoned Montsalvat with the Knight of the Swan,
drained the cup of madness with Hamlet, felt for the first time
a pang whose erotic nature I misunderstood at the time, as
Salome sprawled half-naked over the head of Jokanaan. *Die
Meistersinger* disappointed me, for I expected a tragic story, a
massacre of *"maîtres-chanteurs"* * practicing a kind of racketeer-
ing before their time, or else artists fiercely competing and, toward the end of the performance, cutting each other's throats. As
for *Parsifal,* I was not much interested in the "flower maidens,"
but Amfortas's wound—the cut in his side made by the sacred
spear after he had broken his vow of chastity—disturbed me, and
his lamentations affected me strangely.

I wondered about *Parsifal* most of all, realizing that there was
something to "understand," since my parents spoke of people
who "understood" Wagner and those who "didn't understand";
apparently you had to be not only grown-up but particularly

* A pun, for the words mean "blackmailers" as well as "mastersingers" in
French.—*Translator's note.*

gifted to understand his profound meaning; for me, this became something like the mystery of the Christmas toys and the mystery of birth, something whose meaning I could grasp only vaguely, for the moment, until I grew "old enough to understand it."

Long before I was old enough to go to the theater, I had listened to the stories my sister—thirteen years older than I—told me about the performances she had seen. Best of all had been *Pagliacci,* whose double plot plunged me into an abyss of perplexity: the clown kills his wife in the play, my sister told me, and really kills her too, in front of the spectators who applaud, enchanted by the realism of the actor's performance but convinced that it is only make-believe, whereas the murder is a real one, which they discover only afterward. I did not understand that there was a play within a play, and that these enthusiastic spectators, applauding the murder which takes place before their eyes, were not the real spectators—those in the opera house, including my sister—but spectators played by actors, also in the opera. I thought that each time *Pagliacci* was performed, Tonio actually stabbed his Nedda, and without in the least doubting the authenticity of such behavior, I wondered how such a fantastic thing could be possible. I rid myself of this dilemma by establishing an analogy between this fact and the duels under Louis XIII (which I then considered purely sporting combats, despite their fatal consequences), the combats of gladiators, or the martyrdom of Christians in the circus, which I had also heard about.

The first time I was taken to the theater was to see a magician in the small auditorium of the Musée Grévin. Absorbed by the performance, I neglected to ask my mother to take me out at a convenient time, and forgot myself in my trousers. The odor, and the deep blush that rose to my cheeks, revealed my shame. I don't believe my mother scolded me much, but I was quite mortified by my own stench when she took me home.

Another time we went to the Châtelet to see *Around the World in Eighty Days.* I watched the play quite docilely, and not

even the snakes—though I wondered if they were really alive--
frightened me, nor did the explosion of the boilers on the
steamer *Henrietta;* but going home in the *bateau-mouche* with
my mother and brothers, I was suddenly seized with a fit of panic,
convinced that the boat was going to explode and sink just as the
steamer had, and began to cry and scream: "I don't want it to
blow up . . . I don't want it to blow up . . . ," and refusing to
calm down. Even now I am sometimes tempted to scream such
things to try to stop the march of events: "I don't want there to
be a war!" I would shout, but events seem no more disposed to
obey me than in the past.

By the time I was taken to the opera, I was already too old to
accord events on the stage the same credence as real events—or
inversely, to deduce the nature of real life from what I had seen
on the stage; but I still had a "magical" idea of the theater, conceived of as a world apart, distinct from reality, of course, where
all things, mysteriously arranged in the space which begins beyond the footlights, are transposed to the level of the sublime
and occur in a realm so superior to that of ordinary reality that
the drama developed and unraveled there must be regarded as a
kind of oracle or model. Since the opera seemed to me the pre-
rogative of grownups, and the noblest theater of all, because of
the tragic gravity of what was represented there and the monumental solemnity and pomp with which it was expressed, the
fact of being taken there became a kind of initiation for me, and
I rejoiced in the privilege of being introduced into a milieu regarded as beyond that of my age. I also knew that there were subscribers who were entitled to visit the green room, and that many
of these subscribers had ballerinas for "mistresses" (a word I
have always abhorred because it makes me think of "schoolmis-
tresses").

The performances I was taken to see at the opera, the theater
par excellence of grownups, seemed to me of course the very reflection of their lives (or at least of those among them who were
especially beautiful and privileged) and a glamorous mode of

existence to which, with a certain timidity but from the very depths of my being, I aspired. Hence it was from this period that I acquired a pronounced taste for the tragic, for unhappy love affairs, for everything that ended in misery or in blood. Modeling my image of life on what I saw at the opera and preoccupied above all with love (which I was convinced I could experience without having to be a grownup), I could not conceive of a true passion as other than a life-and-death affair, necessarily ending badly—for if it ended well it would no longer be Love that was as beautiful as the rising of the curtain when you know for sure that it will fall again at the end, the lights will be extinguished and the covers put over the chairs.

The announcement of a performance to which I was to be taken threw me into a fever. I calculated in advance everything that would happen; I learned the names of the singers by heart. I could not sleep the night before, I burned with impatience all day long, but as the hour approached, I gradually felt a touch of bitterness mingled with my joy, and as soon as the curtain rose, a great part of my pleasure left me, for I foresaw that in a little while the performance would be over, and so regarded it as virtually over by the very fact that it had begun. The same is true today of all my pleasures, for I immediately think of death, and I cannot recall those childish regrets in the theater without having to repress a desire to weep.

I rated the opera above all other theater, even the *opéra-comique,* where I had nonetheless seen two performances that had stirred me deeply: *The Flying Dutchman* and *The Tales of Hoffmann.* I shall return, apropos of the former, to the impressions made upon me by its quintessentially romantic hero, a kind of Wandering Jew of the sea, mercilessly pursued by divine punishment. All I shall say about this drama for the moment is that my brothers and I, alone in the house, performed it for a whole day in the vestibule of our apartment (baptized "Théâtre Paris-Lyrique" for the occasion), with improvised sets and costumes; being the youngest, I was given the only female role, that of

Senta, the fisherman's daughter; my older brother played the Dutchman, and one of his friends—the one who had given me the sailboat—old Daland, Senta's father. My part delighted me, as did all the "scapegoat" roles which invariably fell to me when I played with my brothers; hence, when we were in the country (where I had had the revelation of my virility) playing Indians, I was always the prisoner tied to the stake, scalped, and actually frightened out of my wits.

This "scapegoat" aspect, which is one of the profound features of my character, may be linked to the following memory, also of the theater: the terrifying posters for *Children's Prisons,* a realistic play about reform schools, performed at the Ambigu a few years before the war. The poster showed youths with bony, livid faces, wearing wooden shoes and blue berets, guarded by a brutal giant with an enormous belly, huge mustache, and furious eyes. This recollection is no doubt the first to express my profound loathing of the police (physically coarse brutes, stinking of sweat, anally and genitally filthy—much dirtier than workmen who, at least, don't spread such barrack-room stench wherever they go), paralleled by my instinctive fear of criminal types, an ambiguous fear that includes a certain attraction, like the double emotion I felt as I stared at the young prisoners on the poster: insurmountable repugnance, on the one hand, for their pale, criminal faces; pity and sympathy, on the other, because of their misfortune and because I immediately imagined myself as one of them, like the bourgeois hero of the play whose father sends him —for some trifling reason—to reform school and who hangs himself in the last act.

As for *The Tales of Hoffmann,* I was fascinated because there was something to "understand" about the story, pretty much as with *Parsifal.* Three heroines—the doll Olympia, the courtesan Giulietta, the singer Antonia—are presented in three independent tales each of which constitutes an act; at the end, all three, products of Hoffmann's imagination which, under the power of alcohol, has invented all three tales, turn out to be only three images of one and the same woman: the actress Stella, with whom Hoffmann is hopelessly in love. Just before the curtain falls, a huge cask lights up, and in it appears the Muse who sweetly consoles Hoffmann, asleep with his head on the table. This triple incarnation, in various aspects, of an inaccessible woman—in all three cases as well as in reality—must have been one of the first molds in which my notion of the *femme fatale* was formed. An automaton that is broken, a courtesan who betrays, a singer who dies of tuberculosis, such are the avatars through which the contemptuous creature passes in Hoffmann's reverie, changing shape like the Medusa in whom each man believes he recognizes the woman he loves.

This, of course, I perceived only vaguely. I reconstruct it here according to my recollections, adding the observation of what I have subsequently become and comparing these later elements with those earlier ones my memory supplies. Such a method has its dangers, for who knows if I am not attributing to these recollections a meaning they never had, charging them after the fact with an affective value which the real events they refer to utterly lacked—in short, resuscitating this past in a misleading manner?

Here I face the reef on which so many writers of confessions have foundered, and which constitutes a danger I must take into account, if I wish to be objective. I shall therefore confine myself to declaring that I saw everything in life as at the theater, in the light of the performances I was taken to; all things, regarded from a tragic viewpoint, were so colored by the lurid light they cast in my head and heart that even now I cannot love a woman without wondering, for instance, into what drama I might dash for her sake, what torture endure—a grinding of bones or a rending of flesh, drowning or roasting over a slow fire—a question I always answer with so exact an awareness of my terror of physical suffering that I am perpetually crushed by shame, my whole being corrupted by this incurable cowardice.

Such thoughts return to me today with the great image of the Medusa, whose anonymous head above her severed neck illumi-

nates the first part of Goethe's *Faust,* that Faust I first knew in
the stage version of Gounod's librettists, in whose third act he-
who-has-signed-a-pact-with-the-devil sees the apparition of Marguerite with a red ribbon "no thicker than the blade of a knife"
around her neck—a specter I never managed to see at any performance of *Faust,* whatever my efforts and however far I leaned
out over the plush rim of the box, for it glimmered only dimly
and at the right side of the stage.

But other symbolic images of Woman early attracted me, as
diverse as the avatars of Stella in *The Tales of Hoffmann,* fascinating as the Medusa, and as obscure.

Among the most recent, I shall cite Anne Boleyn, who constituted the subject of a curious song I heard last Christmas in London: in a blues rhythm with deliberately lugubrious orchestration, the decapitated woman's misfortunes are celebrated as she
wanders on the Tower and no doubt in the streets as well, "her
head tucked underneath her arm," a stroll which ends in a vulgar
head cold. With Anne Boleyn as well as with Judith I connect,
because of her thin lips, her sharp eyes, and her old-fashioned
servant's uniform, a waitress seen in a restaurant of the Cumber-
land Hotel at the same period.

Earlier symbolic images include Saint Genevieve, Joan of Arc,
and Marie Antoinette, from the period when I still confused the
history of France with Duty and did not suppose there could exist
a female figure more attractive than those of its heroines.

II

Classical Themes

In a bar or night club that resembles Zelli's (a Montmartre dance hall I used to go to regularly) I find myself
in the presence of women who are there not to make
love but to predict the future. They are dressed as
whores usually are. I let myself be dragged in by some of
them, who want to tell my fortune. To do so they evoke
their astral double, which alone is actually clairvoyant.
After various incantations, accompanied by the com-
bustions of certain substances, dances, shrieks, etc., the
astral and true clairvoyants appear. These are women
with beautiful bodies, wearing white linen shifts over
which floats their loose blond hair. Their skin is very
soft and their eyes wild. But instead of noses, all they
have is two little slits only vaguely suggesting nostrils
and, instead of mouths, a little smear of blood. This last
detail proves that they are vampires.

(A dream of July, 1925)

I HAVE always been attracted by *allegories,* enigmatic lessons
in images which often are alluring female figures powerful
in their own beauty and in all that is disturbing, by definition, in a symbol. My sister had initiated me quite early into certain of these mythological representations—such as Truth, rising
naked out of her well, a mirror in her hand, and Deceit, a sump-
tuously dressed woman with a charming smile. I was so fascinated
by this latter apparition, that once when I was talking to my sister about some woman (I no longer recall if she was real or the
heroine of a story), I said: "She's as beautiful as Deceit!"

But there were not only charming allegories, goddesses scantily
clad or richly appareled as nymphs or fairies; there were abstract
and severe ones (like the fable of the peacock Illusion and the
tortoise Experience which I read in *Belles Images,* a story in
which a young prince is accompanied through life by a peacock
whose feathers gradually fade and by a tortoise which, inversely,

grows larger and larger as its shell is encrusted with many jewels),
and even sinister ones (like the story of Poverty, apparently a
Russian legend which I read in an illustrated magazine of the
same kind; a farmer dying of hunger stuffs Poverty, a wizened
old woman, into an empty marrowbone and throws it into a
pond; some lord fishes out the bones or perhaps merely finds the
old woman again and invites her home with him, thus bringing
unhappiness into his own house).

In any case, the word "allegory" was enough to transfigure
everything: whatever the nature of the content expressed (gay or
sad, comforting or terrifying), whatever the aspect of the image
used, the simple fact that there was an allegory was enough to
transfigure everything; all I ever saw was a beautiful statue, as in
the parks, the portrait of a goddess as alluring as Deceit or fair
as Truth. To a large degree, my taste for hermeticism proceeds
from the same impulse as this early love of "allegories," and I
am convinced that it must also be related to my later habit of
thinking in formulas, analogies, images—a mental technique of
which, whether I like it or not, the present account is only an
application.

IN THE *Nouveau Larousse Illustré*, that Bible of adolescence
which—from the age of reason to puberty—I feverishly searched
for answers to the questions raised by sexual curiosity, the
Larousse dictionary (with all its illustrations of attractive allegorical nudes) contains the following appreciation in the article
on Cranach (Lucas) called The Elder (1472–1553):

Cranach resembles Dürer in his understanding of nature, and in
his subtle manner of applying colors, though also achieving vigor-
ous passages; but is distinguished from him by a naïve and child-
like serenity, as well as by a suave and almost timid grace. He is
particularly successful in rendering women's faces. His female
nudes, such as Eve and Lucrece, are very delicate. He frequently
turned to the world of fantasy for the subjects of his masterpieces.

When early in the summer of 1930—looking for a plate of the decapitation of Saint John the Baptist that was to figure in an art review I was working for—I happened to come across the reproduction of a work (moreover a very familiar one) by Cranach which is in the Dresden museum, "Lucrece and Judith," nudes painted on complementary panels, it was not so much the painter's "subtle" qualities that struck me as the eroticism—for me quite extraordinary—which haloes the two figures. The beauty of the models, the two nudes, treated as a matter of fact with extreme delicacy, the classical character of the two scenes, and above all their profoundly cruel aspect (all the more distinct because of their proximity)—everything combined to make this painting particularly suggestive for me, the very type of painting before which one "swoons."

My memory furnishes various elements to illustrate this circumstance, such as the photographs of monuments, busts, mosaics, and bas-reliefs decorating the ancient history text which was my favorite schoolbook during my last year at the *lycée*.

WOMEN OF CLASSICAL TIMES

SINCE childhood I have attributed to everything *classical* a frankly voluptuous character. Marble attracts me by its glacial temperature and its rigidity. I actually imagine myself stretched out on a slab (whose coldness I feel against my skin) or bound to a column. Sometimes it seems to me I could formulate my desire by saying I lusted after a body "cold and hard as a Roman building." The solemnity of the classical style attracts me, and also its bathroom aspect. I think longingly of the Messalina type, the shameless matrons. The idea of Rome, with its banquets, its gladiatorial combats, and its other atrocities of the circus excites me carnally. It is also the image of power. As for Biblical antiquity, I never can think without emotion of Sodom and Gomorrah, those cities destroyed by God's lightning, buried under the Dead Sea that is so thick with bitumen it is almost impossible to drown in it, so that when the Emperor Titus had slaves in chains thrown into it, they were said to have floated on the surface.

One of the words to which I first attributed an erotic value is the word "courtesan," which I understood as the feminine form of the word "courtier," although I sensed there was something special and rather mysterious about it: in all the illustrations, a courtesan wore a Greek peplos, and this always meant an ancient courtesan in the literal sense of the word.

At the age of eleven or twelve, when only the night light was on (I can still see its coppery glow, smell the oil, feel its greasy humidity) and I abandoned myself, in my bed, to solitary pleasures, I performed a slow ceremony which consisted of slipping my nightshirt down over my shoulders in order to free the upper part of my body and have no material anywhere except around my hips, like a loin cloth. Then I imagined myself—as if I had managed to become the object invented and desired—a "courtesan," one of those doubtlessly marginal persons who still had something royal about them, and whose exact social status I was very late in discovering.

HEROIC WOMEN

NOT long ago, I recalled an engraving for *Le Mariage de Roland* from my father's illustrated edition of Hugo's *La Légende des Siècles*. It showed no woman, only Roland and Oliver fighting, helmeted and naked to the waist, shield against shield.

The image of sweating bodies next to the iron of arms and armor, exhaling the same odor as a bronze penny held for a long time in a moist hand (I don't know why I adored this smell): moist, warm skin, over hard muscles, against bronze that was also hot and moist. The armor is shredded by the saber blows; one of the warriors has lost his spurs. No trace of a wound, only the torn metal, the smell of the sweat-drenched bronze. Offstage, "La Belle Aude au Bras Blanc," her splendid white arms emerging from her robe that looks like a nightgown, apparently made of velvet, with a gold clasp on each shoulder. A long, thick robe, probably made of red velvet; white arms naked to the shoulders, and black hair with a narrow diadem, a slender fillet of gold around her forehead; naked feet in coarse leather sandals—very much the diva in a long, vague gown to conceal her opulent figure. The bronze pennies, the bronze armor, the hand moist as though clutching an erect virility; the heat of the sweating rooms, skin beaded with tiny drops, the spirals of steam—everything that happens in Roman baths.

SACRIFICES

In 1927, visiting Olympia during a trip to Greece, I could not resist the desire to offer a libation of a particular kind to the ruins of the Temple of Zeus. I remember that it was a beautiful, sunny day, that there were many sounds of insects, and that the air smelled of pine, and I still see the intimate offering flowing down the soft gray stone. I had the distinct sense—not at all literary, but really spontaneous—that I had offered a *sacrifice,* with all that this word implies of the mystical and the intoxicating.

In the more distant past, I find another example of such a practice accomplished with sacrificial intent. Around the age of puberty, one of my friends and I had instituted a cult in honor of this pagan trinity of our invention: Baïr, Castles, Cauda. The cult was celebrated in my bedroom, and on the marble of the mantelpiece, which served as an altar, were arranged the beer we drank in honor of Baïr, god of alcohol, and the "Three Castles" cigarettes we smoked in honor of Castles, god of tobacco. Only the god Cauda, under a taboo, was not represented. My friend and I committed nothing reprehensible together in honor of this last divinity; it was only when each of us was at home, and alone, that we sacrificed to him.

Perhaps these practices were a little tinged with literature (a predilection for mythology—which a few years earlier had inspired me to draw up tables of concordance for the Greek, Latin, and Germanic pantheons—stories of the Roman orgy type with a vomitorium, or of banquets *à la* Lord Byron where punch was drunk out of skulls). But what is certainly much less "literary" is the fact that during one of these ritual ceremonies we amused ourselves one day by terrorizing my little niece—scarcely more than a baby—by first making the room completely dark, then putting in our mouths matches that had gone out but were still incandescent, and identifying ourselves with terrible divinities of the Moloch variety. We proved ourselves to be child sadists at the same time that we obscurely combined eroticism and fear, a coincidence that has dominated my sexual life as long as I can remember.

Scrutinizing my early childhood—two or three years before I had reached the age of reason—I find the conception of a trinity comparable to that of Baïr, Castles and Cauda which already denoted the same order of "theological" preoccupations. At that period I frequently told my older sister—the mother of the little girl in question—that we would live together, in a house furnished with nothing but white furniture and decorated with only these three images: the Holy Virgin, Joan of Arc, and Vercingetorix, in which trinity the Virgin and Vercingetorix must have been more or less the father and mother and Joan of Arc, perhaps, the hermaphrodite progeny, the warrior Virgin participating in the qualities of both and whom I am tempted to see as anticipating, by her chastity and her murderous strength, those two images of bloody women that stand in my mind today: Lucrece the cold, and Judith the sword-wielder. The furniture reduced to its simplest expression—pure white— already suggests my predilection for severity, in other words my obsession with *punishment,* a phantom that appears to me, in a nightmare of about the same period, in this symbolic form: a storm cloud with the aspect of a judge in a robe and wig. Black clothes to be kept far away from my father's revolver, an American weapon which also represented the law, like the policeman's club hanging in the dining room, a souvenir of my grandfather, who had received it as a gift from the authorities of London during a visit to England.

BROTHELS AND MUSEUMS

TOWARD the end of 1927 or the beginning of 1928, upon my return from that same trip to Greece, I had the following dream:

I am in bed with X who is lying naked on her belly. I admire her back, her buttocks, and her legs, all marvelously white and smooth. Kissing her between her legs I say: "La Guerre de Troie" [The Trojan War]. When I wake up, I think of the word *détroit* [straits] which no doubt explains everything (straits = the declivity of the buttocks).

This phrase "La Guerre de Troie" strongly suggests archeology and museums. And as a matter of fact, museums are almost as powerful a source of pleasure for me as classical antiquity. In a museum of sculpture or painting, it always seems to me that certain forgotten corners must be the scene of hidden lubricity. Another fantasy I have is to surprise and possess a beautiful stranger seen from behind contemplating some masterpiece with a lorgnette; she would remain, apparently, as impassive as a bigot in church or as the professional whore who after having conscientiously performed the job for which you have paid her, leans over the white toilet to empty her defiled mouth, then brushes her teeth vigorously and spits again, with a soft sound that makes you swoon and feel a chill in the marrow of your bones.

Nothing seems more like a whorehouse to me than a museum. In it you find the same equivocal aspect, the same frozen quality. In one, beautiful, frozen images of Venus, Judith, Susanna, Juno, Lucrece, Salome, and other heroines; in the other, living women in their traditional garb, with their stereotyped gestures and phrases. In both, you are in a sense under the sign of archeology; and if I have always loved whorehouses it is because they, too, participate in antiquity by their slave-market aspect, a ritual prostitution.

I discovered this when I was about twelve.

The brother to whom I was closest told me one day how our elder brother—then a student at the School of Decorative Arts—had been taken by a friend to a place called a "portel," a kind of hotel where, my brother said, "You can rent a woman and do anything you want to her." The word "portel," which I must have made up by distorting the original term "bordel," suggested both portal and hotel, and indeed what still seems most moving to me about going to a brothel is the act of crossing a threshold, as one might cast the dice or cross the Rubicon. What I then found scarcely credible about such an institution was the notion of *renting:* to rent a woman as one might rent a hotel room. Probably *buying* a woman would have astounded me less; was I perhaps already familiar with this idea of purchase from the expression "to buy a child," whose erotic undertones I already suspected? But the fact that you could rent a woman and "do anything you want to her," sounded possible only in another world.

At present, what most strikes me about prostitution is its religious character: the pickup or reception ritual, the sameness of the setting, the methodical undressing, the offering of the "present," the rite of the ablutions, and the whore's conventional language, mechanical words whose purpose is so consecrated by usage that it can no longer even be called "calculated," and seems to have existed for all eternity; this moves me as much as the nuptial rites in certain folklores, undoubtedly because it contains the same ancestral and primitive element.

All this must be linked, at least to some degree, to the influence upon me of certain edifying books.

The illustrated works which as an adolescent I surreptitiously removed from my father's bookshelves for inadmissible purposes, were for the most part books which dealt with classical subjects, like Pierre Louÿs' *Aphrodite* and Anatole France's *Thaïs*. Reading Henryk Sienckiewicz's *Quo Vadis* also stirred me deeply, particularly the passage describing a Neronian orgy.

I also recall a colored engraving illustrating a book of tales by Jean Richepin. It showed a naked, black-haired, hard-looking sorceress with powerful hips and beautiful thighs, standing beside a couch of raw, bleeding meat on which she was about to lie down—or make someone else lie down—for a necromantic rite. Perhaps this image is responsible for my notion that prostitution and prophecy are closely related. (I like whores to be superstitious; the sight of a good-looking girl, her breasts hanging out and her face sagging with make-up, telling her fortune with a deck of cards on the corner of a greasy table still pleases me; I'd like to go to brothels as to clairvoyants, perhaps conceiving of destiny in the form of syphilis or gonorrhea.) Perhaps I should simply deduce from this that, for me, the notion of *classical antiquity* is related to that of *nakedness,* provided the latter involves a certain cruelty.

However various the relationships it might suggest, the dream of "La Guerre de Troie," because of the archaism it involves as much as because of its immediately sensual aspect, seems to me to be the ideal image of a scene of prostitution—the site of a sacred spoliation—in all its solemnity. With it, too, is mingled an epic element (since the idea of the "war" is also evoked), and I wonder if it does not thereby express the character of bloody violence which I cannot keep from attributing to the act of intercourse, as in my early childhood when I imagined that children came not from the mother's sex but from her navel—that navel which I had been so startled to learn (at an even earlier period) is, after all, a scar.

THE GENIUS OF THE HEARTH

IF CLASSICAL antiquity is ideally the period when people wore no clothes, it is also, in another aspect, the period when women wore long cymars or robes, like Lucrece or Judith who, when they are not naked, are enveloped in enormous nightgowns.

The room where one of my brothers and I slept was separated from our parents' bedroom by the end of the corridor where there was a dark closet containing old clothes and trunks. Each time that I passed this place, I was afraid—a creature rushing out of the darkness? Weren't there two wolf's eyes gleaming inside? —and it was here that they threatened to lock me up when I was "bad." When my parents had gone to bed, I heard them whispering in their room, where the bed and the other furniture were upholstered in navy blue. They didn't always close the doors between our rooms, opening them again in any case before going to bed, in order to find out how we were sleeping; sometimes I glimpsed my mother as she was preparing for bed, and watched her undress as much as I could; I remember one evening when I secretly debauched myself while staring at her naked breasts.

When I think of my mother, the image of her that comes most frequently is the one I saw then—in a long white nightgown, a braid hanging down her back. That was how she looked, in fact, when I was sick with "false croup," a disease from which I then suffered.

In the middle of the night, I was suddenly awakened by a violent cough which tore through my throat and trachia, seeming to sink deeper and deeper into me, like a wedge or an ax. It hurt, but it also gave me a certain pleasure to wait for the spasms which with each fit of coughing became more violent. I also knew what would follow—the anxiety and the pity my mother would manifest, the care she would lavish on me—and I was vaguely pleased that something had made me *interesting*. I've often enjoyed being sick since then, provided the affliction is not too painful, savoring the sense of irresponsibility—and consequently of total freedom—that sickness gives, the attentions lavished upon me, and also fever itself, with the consequent sensitivity of skin which it produces, a state of tension and sensitivity that are distinctly euphoric.

I was brought into the dining room and my mother took me on her knees, beside the salamander stove which was called La

Radieuse, its trademark. Still crackling with the heat of the embers, La Radieuse was flanked by two tall containers, each holding some ten liters of water whose evaporation, under the influence of the heat, kept the air from getting too dry; the woman's face in the center—a classical effigy on the order of La République—justified the feminine name La Radieuse and made the device into a personification of the domestic hearth. I remember an accident of which the dining room was one day the scene and La Radieuse the chief character. My brother and I wanted to fill her with water, but instead of pouring the liquid into one of the reservoirs, we poured it into the middle orifice, where one ordinarily puts the coal. Naturally the boiling was intense; steam hissed out and glowing coals—violently projected out of La Radieuse's mouth—fell on the floor and charred it. We were delighted and terrified. From that moment on, I believed I understood better the life, hitherto so mysterious, of volcanos; located near the sea, they eject the seething produced by the central fire flooded by infiltrations, and the lava flow scorches the earth as the rain of fire had scorched our floorboards. Another time, the lead stove was moved because the chimney sweeps had come. I remember quite precisely the look of the little sooty boy who was to climb up into the chimney, and the shouts exchanged up and down this terrible acoustical pipe piercing the house from top to bottom, a dizzying tunnel down which God alone knew what might pass, just as down a real tunnel or the neck of a volcano. And this commerce was identified with the riddle of Christmas, which had also employed this obscure channel to deposit the wonderful cache of toys like a kind of magic soot.

When I lolled on my mother's knees near La Radieuse, the stove did not affect me as a monster, but as a warm, kindly animal with a reassuring breath. My mother, who is very short, must have been wearing an old bathrobe over her nightgown with her braid hanging down her back. My father, in a smoking jacket, held the cough medicine, a tiny bottle of brownish liquid which, he said, contained a feather that would tickle my throat and make me vomit. I didn't want to take the emetic, but the idea of the feather intrigued me, as did the circumstance of being the central character in the drama being enacted in the middle of the night, with my mother seated like a Roman matron close to the blue metal of La Radieuse and my father looking for the ipecac among the baroque ornaments of the Henri II sideboard.

DON JUAN AND THE COMMENDATORE

WITHOUT being in any way a bibliophile, I take an almost fetishistic care of my books. Among those to which I am most attached, two are from my mother who received them as prizes or presents, I think, when she was still a young girl:

a Racine, which I particularly like for *Iphigénie* (Clytemnestra battling Agamemnon for the sake of her daughter whom the father is willing to sacrifice; the gods intervening and hurling thunder) and on account of the Racinian versification which affords, along with that classical coldness to which I attach so much value, a kind of intimate suavity in which all the lines become fluid like those of bodies making love;

a Molière, all of whose works I detest for the paltriness they display, with the exception of *Don Juan* (the "grand seigneur as trickster," whose greatness reaches its climax with the terrifying apparition of the Commendatore's statue, white as plaster and hard as antiquity, amid flashes of lightning).

It is in great degree to these two books that I owe my long-standing predilection for a certain classical form, savoring the beautiful lines that emerge with a single burst of energy, like the copulation of an animal or the tension of an obelisk. In a sense, there is no difference for me between "antique" and "classical," since both involve the same purity, hardness, coldness, or inflexibility—whatever one may call it!

The tenderness I transferred from my mother to these books, and from these books as objects to their content, is of a nature to have reinforced the significance I attributed so early to antiquity, as seen from the vantage point of the forbidden shelf in my father's library. These literary recollections have surely contributed to the anguish I felt upon discovering the image of these two heroines, one Roman, the other Biblical: Lucrece and Judith.

III

Lucrece

Lucrece, wife of Tarquinius Collatinus, related to Tarquin the Proud, died 510 B.C.; famous for her tragic
death, which was reputed to have caused the fall of the
Roman royal dynasty. During the siege of Ardea, the
princes of the royal family desired to learn how their
wives were behaving in their absence. They called for
their horses, rode to Rome that night, and found their
wives diverting themselves quite frivolously. Only Lucrece was spinning wool at home, surrounded by her
women. Her beauty made a profound impression upon
Sextus Tarquin. A few days later, he returned to Rome,
appeared at Lucrece's house, requested hospitality, and
after entering her apartments late at night, threatened
to kill her if she resisted him, and to spread the rumor
that he had killed her because she was betraying her
husband; Lucrece yielded; but summoning her father
and husband the next morning, she told them of the
outrage she had suffered and killed herself before their
eyes with a dagger. Brandishing the bloody dagger,
Julius Brutus incited the Roman people to revolt, and
the fall of the Tarquins was proclaimed.

(*Nouveau Larousse Illustré*,
after Livy)

To DESCRIBE the erotic act—or rather the couch which is
its theater—I should prefer to use the expression "terrain
of truth" which is the bullfighting term for the arena, the
site of the combat. Just as the matador or "death-dealer" gives the
measure of his value when he finds himself face to face and alone
with the bull (that circumstance which bullfighting slang characterizes so well by saying that he is "confined"), so in sexual relations, confined face to face with the partner whom he must domi-
nate, man discovers himself confronting a reality. I who suffer
enormous difficulties in facing events, and who, save when I am
afraid, have the impression of floundering in the vaguest possible
unreality, I am a fervent admirer of bullfights, for more than at

the theater—and even more than at the circus, where everything is lessened by being identically repeated, anticipated, and stereotyped each evening whatever the danger—I have the impression of watching something real: a ritual death, a *sacrifice* more valid than any strictly religious sacrifice, because here the sacrificer is constantly threatened with death, and with a bodily catastrophe—being caught on the horns—instead of the magical, i.e., fictional disaster which threatens anyone entering into too abrupt a contact with the supernatural. It is not essential to know whether the *corrida* derives from the Cretan tauromachy, from the cult of Mithra, or from some other religion in which bulls were destroyed, but merely to determine why it assumes this sacrificial quality which—much more than its immediately sadistic interest—gives the *corrida* an emotional value insofar as the presence of something sacred causes a disturbance that involves the sexual emotion.

The whole *corrida* is presented, first of all, as a kind of mythical drama, whose subject is as follows: the Beast mastered, then killed, by the Hero. The moments when the divine is present—when the sense of a catastrophe perpetually invoked and avoided creates a rapture in whose depths horror and pleasure coincide—are those moments when the *torero* plays with death, escaping it only miraculously, charming it; thereby he becomes the hero, incarnating the crowd which attains through him to immortality, to an eternity all the more intoxicating for hanging by only a thread.

As for the beast, there is the notion of its fatal condemnation, the complicity—or communion—of the spectators who participate in this murder, who acclaim or jeer the matador depending on whether he is great enough for them to identify themselves with him, who encourage him with their *olés!* that are not a reward but an assistance of the kind one might give to a woman in childbirth by groaning oneself.

Lured from cape to pike, from pike to the man who turns into a cape, from man to *banderilla*, from *banderilla* to sword, and from sword to dagger, the huge beast is soon no more than a mountain of steaming flesh. If there were only this murder decorated with more or less attractive flourishes, the *corrida* would not have that superhuman beauty based on the fact that between matador and bull (the beast wrapped in the cape that deceives it, the man wrapped in the bull that turns around him) there is a union along with the combat—as there is in love and in sacrificial ceremonies, in which there is close contact with the victim, fusion of officiants and observers in this animal that will be their ambassador to the powers of the other world and—in most cases—actual absorption of its substance by the eating of its dead flesh.

It would certainly be difficult to interpret the present ceremony of the *corrida* as the direct survival of a cult, for we know that the *corrida* was originally a manifestation of chivalry, like the tournaments; that before Pedro Romero, Costillares, and Pepe Hillo, professional *toreros* who elaborated the code of modern bullfighting toward the beginning of the nineteenth century, the entire function was much cruder. Still, various facts may be enlisted which curiously support the thesis of its sacrificial significance.

First of all, there is the coincidence of the great bullfights with local *fiestas*, which correspond to religious festivals. Then there is the use of special brilliantly decorated costumes, called "suits of light," which figure as sacerdotal ornaments and transform the protagonists into a kind of clergy. Even the *coleta*, a small (now artificial) braid the *toreros* wear as a sign of their profession, suggests the tonsure of priests.

Examining more deeply, we cannot fail to be struck by the extreme precision of the etiquette, especially with regard to killing the bull. On the part of the performers, we note that contrary to the rules of sport, which specify a great number of permissible plays and a limited number of forbidden plays, the bullfighting code allows the "player" only a very small number of permissible "plays" in relation to the considerable number of forbidden ones; hence, one might imagine one was watching not a sporting event, whose rules constitute merely a loose framework, but a magical operation with a meticulously calculated development, in which questions of etiquette and style take precedence over immediate effectiveness. On the part of the public, we note that the bull's death occurs in an atmosphere of distinct solemnity. Whether the matador is acclaimed for working bravely and artistically as well, or derided for not having killed but merely slaughtered; whether the bull is applauded for its bravery or jeered for its cowardice, the fact remains that the public's attitude at this moment is a religious attitude toward the death the creature has suffered, as might be proved by the fact that in certain *plazas* everyone stands as soon as the animal has fallen, and sits down again only for the next animal's entrance into the ring. Furthermore, there is a custom such as the *alternative*, the investiture of the new matador by one of his elders, as a lord might arm a knight; and the ceremony of dedicating the bull which he is about to kill to a personality in the audience, to the entire public, or to the city in which the festival is taking place (so that the bull thus offered constitutes, strictly speaking, the *victim*); or even a procedure such as the consumption of the genitals of the sacrificial beast, an apparently recent custom which certain fanatical *aficionados* practice, being served in their seats while watching the other bullfights and thus enjoying organs of the dead bull in a kind of ritual feast, as if they intended to assimilate its *virtù*.

The bullfight's magical character is intimately linked with this quality of a religious ceremony (more valid than those of Western religions, which have lost their profound meaning by countenancing sacrifice only in a symbolic form), and in order to be affecting, I believe it is relatively unimportant whether a bullfight is technically good or bad; the point is that there be the killing of an animal according to precise laws, and mortal danger for the man who does the killing. Of the six bullfights I have seen so far, the first, in the Roman arena of Fréjus, was quite ignominious: *toreros* either too young or too old; huge calves mas-

sacred more crudely than in the slaughterhouse, sometimes low-
ing or urinating in terror; the crowd showing off in order to behave in what they assumed was a Spanish manner; the president
of the bullfight according the tail of one creature that had been
put to death less clumsily than the rest, and the matador to
whom this undeserved distinction had fallen gallantly tossing
the tail to a spectator in the boxes; this lady fainting, her friends
reviving her, wrapping the trophy in a newspaper and trying to
make her understand the delicacy of the intention.

The second (a "sham" fight in French Catalonia, at Saint-
Laurent de Cerdan) was absurd but touching: *sardañas* danced
to celebrate the occasion in the village square—where the bullfight itself took place—under the sunny clamor of wind instruments called *tenoras;* hotel windows turned into boxes, with
shawls hanging from the sills; *aficionados* getting themselves
trampled for the glory of snatching the cockades (the best at this
was a butcher boy); taking up a collection to replace one *torero*'s
trousers that had been ripped by a thrust of the horn.

The third, at Saragossa, was a *novillada*—a regular bullfight,
but with young or spoiled bulls not suited to perform in a formal
corrida. Its mediocrity as a cut-rate spectacle did not prevent it
from being fascinating: a man named Fidel Cruz was tossed
twice on the horns, but came back to the bull green in the face
and finally made a good *descabello,* a thrust in the back of the
neck which dispatches the bull by severing its spinal marrow.
One frightened animal jumped virtually into the audience. A
very young matador from Seville whose cape work was superb
was hissed out of the ring after having correctly killed an unfortunately weak animal whose removal from the ring the public
had demanded in vain; he finished his work under a hail of seat
cushions and then, his adversary dispatched, left the ring supported by his friends, sobbing into his *biretta.* There was an in-
termission for a lottery which was held in the middle of the
arena, where the numbers were drawn out of a barrel stirred up
by a crank; the occasion was ended by a police charge, with gun

butts raised, for the crowd had filled the ring after the incident from which the young Andalusian had suffered.

The fourth took place in Barcelona, at the Monumental, a plaza covered with posters, like a kind of Spanish Vel' d 'Hiv'; two matadors—one Mexican and the other Basque—worked as well as they could with difficult animals. No one thought it strange that the Red Cross Band should be used as the orchestra; the bullfighting was painful and dangerous, but consistently lackluster and grim. The last two I saw last summer; one in Victoria—with Joaquin Rodriguez Cagancho (an arrogant gypsy as famous for his grace as for his frequent fits of panic), Pepe Bienvenida (whose style is delicate and classical), Luis Gomez El Estudiante (a slender and aristocratic medical student, straight as a reed, who had transferred his interest to bullfighting), Luis Castro El Soldado (a Mexican of remarkable courage, and a savage *torero*)—the other in Valencia, with Rafael Ponce Rafaelillo ("little Rafael"), a local boy whom the press unanimously hailed as a prodigy. The latter two bullfights were admirable in every detail; they roused my enthusiasm, of course, yet they revealed nothing that notably modified my point of view. And at all my *corridas,* except that which was performed without a killing, I was moved to almost the same degree. It is therefore not the spectacle that is essential but the sacrifice, the precise gestures performed on the brink of death and in order to inflict death.

WHEN I go to a bullfight, I tend to identify myself with either the bull at the moment the sword is plunged into its body, or with the matador who risks being killed (perhaps emasculated?) by a thrust of the horn at the very moment when he most clearly affirms his virility.

The image of Lucrece in tears after being raped by her brother-in-law, the soldier Sextus Tarquin, is therefore an image ideally suited to affect me. I cannot conceive of love save in torment and tears; nothing moves or attracts me so much as a woman weeping, unless it is a Judith with murderous eyes. Look-

ing back to my earliest childhood, I find memories connected
with stories of *wounded women*.

MY UNCLE THE ACROBAT

MY MOTHER, when I was still very young (it was a period when
she came to my room and bathed me every morning), had given
lodging to her brother, who was suffering from a fractured wrist
and had no one to take care of him, having just separated from
his wife and possessing means much too modest to enable him to
hire a nurse. One morning when she was carrying me in her
arms, she went into my uncle's room in order to dress his wrist,
slipped, and fell down hard. Her head, unfortunately, struck the
corner of a piece of furniture and bled profusely. My uncle, unable to hold her up because of his arm, which was in a sling, ob-
served the scene helplessly, swearing and calling for help. As for
me, I shrieked like a stuck pig, having fallen on my chin and
hurt myself—badly enough so that moving my jaws was painful
for several days afterward.

The uncle in question, my mother's brother whose broken
wrist had been the accident's first cause, is a character who had a
great influence upon me. Because of what he represented in my
eyes, and perhaps too because of his relationship to my mother, I
always loved him, contrary to the relatives on my father's side,
whom I have almost always detested. Though he was the son of a
high police official endowed with all the bourgeois Puritanism of
a *"républicain de '48,"* my uncle, in his way a respectable person
(at the period when I knew him, he went to church every week,
but on *Wednesdays,* so as not to be bothered by the Sunday
crowd), led a scandalous life in comparison to the milieu in
which he had been raised.

Stage-struck and endowed with remarkable comic gifts, he
first studied to be an actor, intending to join the Théâtre Français; but he was disgusted by the pontificating hams with whom
he was obliged to work, and began acting in cloak-and-dagger

melodramas in provincial and neighborhood theaters. Finding even this medium too artificial and fraudulent, he became a café-concert singer, then a circus juggler. Only here did he feel comfortable, among people who were genuinely simple and honest, dedicated body and soul to their art.

At the very time of this transformation—which could only be a "failure" for his bourgeois circle—he climaxed a turbulent erotic life by a ridiculous marriage, and then by a still more ridiculous affair, preferring to women who were superior to them in every regard two stupid cows of whom the first—a farm girl who had run away from her family with a troupe of Chinese circus performers—had been a sword-swallower, then a rope-dancer. Her beautiful body fascinated my uncle, who had her "under his skin"; but he was finally disgusted by her bestial sensuality, especially since she suffered at being older than he and tormented him beyond endurance with her jealousy. My earliest memory of her is in a dress so red that she looked as if she had been dipped in fresh blood. The concubine who succeeded her was ugly, of an almost revolting grossness, and, if possible, even more stupid than the first. She tortured my uncle with incessant teasing and ridicule.

My mother was very fond of her brother, and I often heard her and my father discussing his "Don Quixote" character. For years, he came to our house for dinner every week—every *Monday,* if I remember correctly. Often he took me to the music hall, and as a past master explained all the acts to me; in many cases, for instance, he knew how many people in Europe could perform the feat we were watching; he taught me to appreciate the difference between real mastery and what were nothing but vulgar tricks for effect. Sometimes, too, he took me with him to visit his old colleagues, all circus or music-hall performers; I recall among others a family of tumblers making a living as truck gardeners in a hut beyond the city limits. In the little apartment my uncle occupied in the outskirts of Paris there was a table covered with all the materials of juggling: red and white rings, cannonballs, wands of various shapes, clubs, top hats. Although he did not perform any longer for the public, he juggled every morning, as a kind of calesthenics; frequently he performed for me, and his skill seemed miraculous. Very emaciated, his nose prominent, he looked indeed like a kind of wretched strolling player out of *Don Quixote*. During our sister's pregnancy, in order to indicate the difference in value which she and our uncle represented in our eyes, my brother and I devised the practice of calling the double-six domino "Juliette," the double-one "Uncle Léon."

Despite his age, his complete lack of snobbery, and the retired life he led, my uncle had a sense of topical interest that was occasionally quite remarkable; for instance, it was he who told me about Chaplin's films when they were first shown, during the war, assuring me that the world had just witnessed the advent of a clown of extraordinary genius. Certain precepts he repeated to me have remained fixed in my mind, and I still subscribe to them: in particular he made me understand that the perfection of a song or of a music-hall routine may require a great deal more talent than more ambitious performances. It was he, too, who taught me that there can be "more poetry in an organ-grinder's song than in a classical tragedy."

Without attempting to compare myself to him in matters of temperament or courage, I feel very close to this uncle who sought all his life, with admirable consistency, what to others was only *abasement*. He found his wife in the sawdust, his mistress virtually in the street, so strong was his predilection for the simple and the authentic, which he felt he could find only among such humble people. Great, too, must have been his delight in *self-sacrifice*—here he was very much like myself, who have so long sought (and at the same time feared), in different forms, suffering, failure, expiation, punishment.

The prestige of this uncle was even greater in my eyes because he had frequented almost every level of society—including the worst, and because in his youth a woman he had wanted to leave had stabbed him with a knife.

His death, like my father's (which occurred some years later), coincided with a heavy snowfall. All his life he had never been able to see snow falling without feeling a kind of dizziness.

EYES PUT OUT

AT THE AGE of six or seven, playing with a Eureka carbine, I one day accidentally shot a dart into the eye of the servant-girl my parents employed. The girl (her name was Rosa, and she was quite promiscuous) rushed off screaming that I had put out her eye.

I don't believe servant-girls ever particularly excited me (except perhaps for two: a German girl whom my brothers and I had for some reason named "Éclair," and later, vacationing with my parents at an English seaside resort, one of the hotel chambermaids). I therefore consider it doubtful that the event I have just related had any specially ambiguous value for me; but I remember how I sobbed and cried at the idea of having put out this girl's eye.

Another disagreeable aspect of an "eye put out" was my suffering at the age of ten or eleven during a game my sister and her husband made me play. This is how it was played.

You blindfold the one who is "it" and tell him you're going to make him "put someone's eye out." You lead him, index finger extended, toward the supposed victim, who is holding in front of his eye an egg cup filled with moistened bread crumbs. At the moment the forefinger penetrates into the sticky mess, the supposed victim screams.

I was "it," and my sister the victim. My horror was indescribable.

The significance of the "eye put out" is very deep for me. Today I often tend to regard the female organ as something dirty, or as a wound, no less attractive for that, but dangerous in itself, like everything bloody, mucous, and contaminated.

PUNISHED GIRL

IN THE very conservative institution where I first went to school,
a certain number of students (most of them selected among the
older children) were chosen to act out a little religious play
about the Nativity, on the occasion of the Christmas holidays or
the distribution of prizes. This play presented in several short
scenes the various wonders in the pagan world that heralded the
birth of Jesus Christ. It ended with the Adoration of the Magi
and the Shepherds. Aside from the final one, the only two scenes
I remember are as follows:

In one, the chief character was a Greek sailor who heard a
voice speaking over the waters, proclaiming the death of Pan and
thereby announcing the passing of the old gods;

the other concerned a vestal virgin condemned to be buried
alive for allowing the sacred fire to go out (a torture which I
later learned was also the punishment for those who violated
their vows of chastity); it was a young boy—pale and delicate as
could be, and whose name, I think, had a particle in it—who
played the vestal virgin.

During the entire performance, and particularly in the scene
when a young girl was to be put to death, I suffered from the
excitement always aroused in me by classical antiquity, whose
symbol is rigidity of fate. As a matter of fact, the performance
came particularly close to this image of Destiny, for it ended suddenly with the intervention of Jupiter Tonans: a large quantity
of magnesium exploded into a conflagration which sent the
whole audience to join the Adoration of the Shepherds.

From this same school (where I enrolled again during the war,
to prepare my second *baccalauréat*) I was expelled several times,
on the pretext—I was then seventeen—that instead of studying I
was encouraging my fellow pupils to get drunk in the bars frequented by aviators; actually, they were merely following my
example without any active propaganda on my part. Each of

these dismissals was revoked, for I always managed to vanquish the principal—a chauvinistic Alsatian with a long gypsy mustache that made my mother say he looked like a *Rasta* (an adventurer)—either because he had admired my edifying attitude during Mass (which we were obliged to attend every Thursday morning) or because I made the promise—without any intention of keeping it—to enlist in the army in order to "redeem" myself.

Toward the end of the war, boys older than I who enlisted after a dissolute life were adorned in my eyes, without the slightest patriotic sentiment being involved in such a reaction, with the halo of those whom a severe chastisement permits to "redeem themselves," provided they have deliberately sought out their punishment.

MARTYRED SAINT

AROUND the period of my first Communion, I attended a school run by a priest (an old snuff-dipper with a face like a Spanish corsair, who came from Roussillon, and who administered severe punishments in the forms of pinches when we behaved badly) and received as a prize Cardinal Wiseman's novel *Fabiola*. This book, a narrative of the horrors the Christians suffered during the Roman persecution, describes the martyrdom—with illustrations in appropriate places—of a young virgin who is tortured by being tied to a rack and having her arms and legs broken, one after the other. I did not read the whole of the insipid novel, but I was absolutely enthralled by this episode. I can still see the martyr's convulsed face, her long hair, and her bare feet bruised by the ropes; I believe she was a girl of the people, dressed in a wretched tunic, and surrounded by brutal centurions and legionnaires. A wooden wheel served to draw the cords tighter.

This recollection goes with the older but more precise one (for I returned to the place, with what emotion! about seven years ago) of a walk with my mother, when I was still very young, to the Musée Grévin.

As well as a painting of the Russo-Japanese War—the siege of Port Arthur, I think, in the foreground the body of a Japanese soldier with a bullet through his temple, an image of slaughter that haunted me for a long time—I saw the famous catacombs, the naked Christians behind the grill separating them from the lions to which they were promised, and the beautiful wax figure of a woman, naked and life-size, nursing or holding in her arms a child half covered by her beautiful hair, whose heavy black curtain fell down her back and over her breasts, which the lions' fangs would soon rend and drain of their blood and milk. Instinctively, I identified myself with the Christians, and I was as frightened of the crudely painted lions in the background as of the wax statues, mummified corpses that were somehow desirable, with their naked, impassive, pink flesh.

The impressions of a very substantial nature which I experienced at the sight of this pious spectacle as upon the partial reading of *Fabiola* in no way contradict the presence within me of a certain degree of mysticism. I made what was called a "fervent" first Communion, or nearly that. I expected a miracle, a fabulous revelation at the moment the Eucharist dissolved in my mouth. I also was afraid to swallow it, knowing that it was too big for my throat, and unaware it could melt like a pill or capsule; I also feared spitting it out once I did manage to swallow it, unless God intervened and made it dissolve, a miracle analogous to that of the Christmas toys which, whatever their dimensions, managed to reach the bottom of the chimney. I was horribly disappointed in my expectation as in my fear (scarcely more, though as much, as during my erotic initiation). Telling myself: "That's all it is" and no longer hoping for a miracle, I soon ceased to be a communicant, then to believe, and I have never begun again.

HOWEVER vivid these various recollections, characterized by the presence in each of a Lucrece, i.e., a woman either wounded or punished, they pale beside those which relate to dangerous women, i.e., to versions of Judith.

IV

Judith

Judith, a Hebrew heroine whose story is told in the book of the Old Testament that bears her name. In substance, it runs as follows: the city of Bethulia, besieged by the army of Holofernes, a general of Nebuchadnezzar, King of Nineveh, is about to capitulate. A widow named Judith, resolved, by God's inspiration, to save her people, leaves the city with a single servant-girl and makes for the camp of the Assyrians. Taken to Holofernes' tent, she captivates him by her beauty, agrees to sit at his table, and when he is overcome by drunkenness, cuts off his head with his own sword and returns to Bethulia during the night. The next day, the Jews hang Holofernes' bleeding head on their walls, and the Assyrians, terrified, raise the siege after having suffered a bloody defeat.

(Nouveau Larousse Illustré,
after the Book of Judith)

I CANNOT say, strictly speaking, that *I die,* since—dying a violent death or not—I am conscious of only part of the event. And a great share of the terror which I experience at the idea of death derives perhaps from this: bewilderment at remaining suspended in the middle of a seizure whose outcome I can never know because of my own unconsciousness. This kind of unreality, this *absurdity* of death, is (without taking into account the physical suffering by which it might be accompanied) its radically terrible element, and not, as some may think *("Après moi le déluge!"* "Since there's nothing after death, why are you afraid?" "What's the difference to you, since you won't be here any more?" etc. . . .), what might make it acceptable.

It is natural, from this point of view, for people to write their wills, compose their epitaphs, decide on the ceremony of their funerals, take comfort in the fact that mourning will be worn for them, and all such things likely to convince them they will continue, in a certain degree, to exist. If there is anything repugnant about this, it is the kind of *assurance* displayed, the factitious and purely social, conventional character of such assurance and above all the lack of taste—in fact, the bad manners—that it represents, for who would want to associate other people so intimately with the corruption of one's own cadaver?

In another way, one might say that the seizure of death has an analogy with the sexual spasm, of which one is never conscious, strictly speaking, because of the collapse of all the faculties which it implies and because of its character as a momentary return to chaos. The well-known sadness after coitus derives from this same delirium inherent in any unresolved crisis, since in the sexual involvement as in death the climax is accompanied by a loss of consciousness, at least partial in the former case. If love is often conceived of as a means of escaping death—or denying it or, in practical terms, forgetting it—this is perhaps because we somehow sense that it is the only means we have for experiencing death to whatever degree, for in coitus at least we know what happens afterward and can witness—however dismayed—the consequent disaster. Love may also be a means of magical action: to ward off an evil fate, to evade the sordid incident that threatens us by articulating it on a smaller scale and deliberately, as though settling a bill as cheaply as possible, sacrificing the part to be rid of the whole. This same "magical" behavior, which consists of intentionally doing what we are afraid of in order to deliver ourselves from it, is also exemplified in suicide, which in many respects derives its prestige from the fact that it appears to us, paradoxically, as the only means of escaping death by making use of it at will, by creating it ourselves. But, in committing suicide, we do not cut our losses; we fling ourselves into the abyss altogether —without remission.

Such are the reflections which come to my mind now that I am to speak about Judith.

The story of Judith—a heroine terrible twice and three times over because, first a widow, she becomes a murderess, and a murderess of the man with whom, the moment before, she has gone to bed—did not move me especially when as a small boy I first read it in the little book called *Sacred History* where it was told. It is true that every licentious detail had been scrupulously removed. Much more exciting for me was the story of the Maccabees, their battles and the tortures which, under the eyes of their mother, several of them suffered. Yet Judith, who cut off her lover's head with his own sword, then wrapped that head in a veil or put it in a sack to carry it away, is a figure around which are crystallized the images that had a decisive influence upon my life.

AS FAR back as I can remember—and no doubt before my birth —there was, in my parents' house, an engraving in detestable taste showing the famous episode of the "Lion in Love": at the edge of a kind of grotto or cavern sits a naked woman, with her hair gathered up into a chignon toward the top of her head, bending lovingly over an enormous lion that looks completely stupefied.

What strikes me about this engraving is not so much the danger incurred by the woman of being clawed to death as the stupidity of the lion, a huge male who is letting himself be trifled with. I also see it as a sign of my father's bad taste.

I've been told that a man whom I knew, and who committed suicide, recalled having conceived a lasting hatred of his father the first day he heard him fart. The hostility I feel toward my own father derives in particular from his inelegant physical aspect, from his cheery vulgarity, and from his total absence of taste in all artistic matters.

Possessing an agreeable tenor voice, he sang arias by Massenet, and this sentimental sensuality exasperated me. It never occurred to me that anything really *erotic* could occur between him and my mother.

Regarding his broker's career as an absurdity (and I now consider his scorn for his profession as one of the good sides of his character), he had dreamed of artistic careers for his two older sons: the first was to be a decorator, the second a violinist; as for me, I was destined for the École Polytechnique. . . . Poor man! Destiny has indeed deceived him: at present, my elder brothers are both brokers and I am the only one who might, at best, be considered an "artist."

Sometimes, to decorate our home, my father purchased absolutely hideous statues. Three of them seem particularly characteristic to me.

The first two are terra-cotta busts executed in a modern style and representing women suggestive of sirens, nymphs, or even walkyries. The third is an enormous bronze of a snake-charmer. Holding a long slender trumpet to her lips, her delicate shoulders swathed by the serpent's coils, the snake-charmer is completely naked except for her head, which is embellished by a turban. I can still hear my father saying to one of his friends, who was congratulating him on this acquisition: "What's really lovely about the piece is that, although she's naked, she's very chaste all the same." Yet I have more than once indulged in contestable behavior because of this statue, having first fingered the entire body at great length.

My father was a very kindly, affable, and fundamentally generous man. He enjoyed entertaining and, insofar as his means allowed, indulged himself as a Maecenas. A fervent enthusiast of singing, he organized a series of musicales at home, where the artists he knew performed. Among other persons, he often invited to dinner along with her husband (my mother's second cousin, a brilliant and sympathetic man who enjoyed good food and comfortable living, but who was subsequently to die in horrible agony of an anal cancer) a Flemish soprano quite famous at the period. My sister, my brothers, and I regarded her as an aunt (although she was only a cousin by marriage), and I shall designate her here under the pseudonym of "Tante Lise." Simple and kindly despite her imposing physique, Tante Lise was a robust and strapping woman, of extraordinary health and endowed

with a splendid voice. I can still see her, calm as a heifer in her
not very pretty but extraordinary gowns, with her lovely round
arms, her fleshy hips, her heavy breasts, her black hair, her red
lips, her fresh skin, and her superb eyes that were always too
dark, for she had no sense at all of how to put on her make-up.

Of her private life I can remember virtually nothing. At the
period when she came to sing at my parents' house and later,
when I was an adolescent, I never saw her save under the typical
aspect of the "woman of theater," which is to say that the only
thing in her life that mattered to my eyes was her life on the
stage. I know, however, that a few years after her widowhood,
her jewels and various other objects were stolen from her by a
devoted maid in whom she had long placed all her trust. During
the war I was to see her only twice: once at our house, when she
came to dinner with her nephew, a boy over six feet tall who
served as an aviator in the Belgian army; once in a street near
the Madeleine, where I encountered her with a Balkan diplomat,
a great Francophile wearing a bowler and clothes of scrimped
elegance.

But I had heard her or seen her photograph in various roles
almost all of which have this in common: that, from my childhood, they made her a Judith.

CARMEN

CARMENCITA—who stabs one of her companions in the cigar
factory and ridicules until he kills her the wretch whom she has
forced to desert; mistress of a matador ("Remember! Yes, remember when you fight, that a pair of black eyes are watching
you, and that love awaits you!") who dedicates to her the beast
he is about to kill, as to a bloodthirsty goddess for whom he
must risk death—the lovely Carmencita, before being murdered,
is indeed a murderess. A thrilling role, in which Tante Lise appeared to me as a magnificent and tempting creature, quite
closely related to the bullfights, whether she was sitting in a chair

with her arms tied behind her back, teasing Don José into letting
her go, or in the third act in the mountains when—docilely telling her fortune among these smugglers who, among their con-
traband, might (I no longer remember) even have carried blun-
derbusses—she sees with terror the card "Death! Again! Always!
Death!" and becomes as obsessive as fatality itself, from the mere
fact that she has been able to discern its approach.

LA GLU

I saw Tante Lise in the role of Marie-des-Anges in this miserable operetta based on Richepin's novel. The scenario is pure
reportage: a fisherman's widow kills the village flirt who has
seduced and then jilted her son; the vamp's ex-husband—a doctor—gives himself up in order to save the guilty woman.

In this role, Tante Lise appeared in a Breton peasant's coif
(which, above her fat and heavily made-up face, had nothing particularly suitable about it). Her great success was the famous
"Chanson du Coeur" which moved me to the highest degree. It
tells of a son captivated by a strumpet who asks him for "his
mother's heart to give her dog"; having killed his mother and
brought her bleeding heart to the strumpet, the son stumbles and
falls; then we hear the heart saying: "Did you hurt yourself, my
child?"

What struck me most in this drama was the *good* mother opposed to the *bad* mistress, like the briny ocean opposed to the
rainy city where the vamp was languishing. In the second act,
La Glu sang her own aria: the mortal boredom of a heartless
bitch, idle, insatiable, actually frigid, vainly seeking to fill the
void of her dissatisfaction. More than the old Marie-des-Anges
who smashes her skull with a tremendous blow of a marlin-spike,
she is Judith, although the other woman is the executioner and
she the victim.

SALOME

I HAVE seen several photographs of Tante Lise in the role of
Richard Strauss's *Salome*. I was completely dazzled by the spectacle of her powerful breasts confined by two discs of chased
metal, over her naked flesh or over pink body tights, and it
seemed to me I could even smell her body.

This drama, the whole of which takes place on the Tetrarch
Herod's terrace overlooking a Dead Sea still impregnated with
the rain of fire and brimstone that annihilated Sodom and
Gomorrah, cities destroyed by the wrath of God, has always
given me, as much by Strauss's music as by Oscar Wilde's text,
an impression of nightmare, of agonizing eroticism. The anxious
Tetrarch who fears bad omens ("Ha! I have slipped in blood!")
and seeks a refuge in debauchery, and on the other hand Salome
crushed—by order of the twice-incestuous Tetrarch—under the
soldiers' shields (after having played with a head which, by her
request, the Tetrarch has ordered to be cut off for her), are quite
hallucinatory elements. I have often more or less identified myself with this cowardly and cruel Tetrarch rolling drunk at
Salome's feet.

As a child, I saw Strauss's *Salome* twice, at the opera. The first
time, with the Italian soprano Gemma Bellincioni, who quite
properly accentuated the character's morbid side; the second
time, with the Scottish soprano Mary Garden, then a very beautiful woman. On several occasions, I stimulated my imagination
with a photograph of this glamorous soprano, showing her in a
long close-fitting sequined tunic that outlined the mount of
Venus and left one arm, shoulder, and armpit entirely naked.

More recently, I have seen the Wilde *Salome* with Georges
Pitoëff as Herod and his wife as Salome. It was toward the end of
an affair I shall discuss later, and I felt terribly sad at seeing this
play with a woman whom I had already ceased to love. During
this same affair, and perhaps around the same period, feeling my

love diminish and wanting to punish myself for it, I had gone into my bathroom naked and, with a kind of furious and voluptuous determination, had lacerated my whole body with the points of my nail-scissors.

Finally, on the evening of December 17, 1934, I saw *Salome* again at the opera, which I had not visited for a long time. An English soprano sang the role of the perverse child, a Wagnerian tenor with an enormous belly and pectorals sang the role of Herod, an Australian baritone with a country Hercules face played the skeletal Jokanaan. I had not remembered how extraordinarily and continuously vehement Strauss's orchestration was. The Englishwoman sang quite well, but was completely lacking in any plastic sense; moreover, she was far too elaborately dressed, swathed in heavy, rigid stuffs; her contortions had nothing arousing about them, and as a strip-tease her Dance of the Seven Veils was a cheat. As always at the opera, the actors seemed tiny (wedged between the enormous stage with its icy draughts and the pit boiling with whitish plastrons and hairy heads) and virtually nothing of what they were singing could be understood. But the Tetrarch's frenzy (conventional, however grotesque, in its melodramatic style) situated the work on what remains, for me, its true level: the story of an obsessed, erotomaniac monarch who sees death everywhere and is convulsed at the sight of Woman, trembling at the prophet's words intoned from the bottom of his pit like a voice rising, out of space and time, from the depths of the uterus; when he sees, at the end, that things are quite beyond his control, he orders the woman to be killed, stamping like a child whose toys will no longer pay any attention to him.

There is a great deal to be said about this drama and about Salome herself, an implacable and castrating child (she demands the severed head of the prophet, although she loves him; furthermore, another man, almost at the beginning of the play, disembowels himself for her) finally punished by Herod, an incestuous and terrified father. From the curtain's rise until its fall,

everything happens in the stormy order of the *sacred,* without
relief, among the smells of the bazaar mingled with the clatter of
penny-arcade peep-show machines.

ELECTRA, DELILAH, AND FLORIA TOSCA

In *Comœdia Illustré* or *Musica* appeared a portrait of Tante
Lise as she appeared in the *Elektra* Richard Strauss composed to
a libretto by von Hofmannsthal: barefoot, hair wild, brandishing a lighted torch in a frenzied dance.

Electra belongs to the cycle of tragedies indissolubly linked
in my mind with my mother's copy of Racine. Her muscular
legs, her intensity, her laugh, her flaming torch, her loose hair
suggest the typical bacchante, with something darker, however,
as remote from the rustic dancers crowned with vine leaves as is,
for instance, one of our harvest banquets from a ritual intoxication among the African tribes.

I remember having heard my father say that Tante Lise had
ruined her voice singing this role, because of the savage violence
it required and because of the many cruel vocal leaps called for
in the score.

Many times I heard her sing Delilah's great aria from *Samson
and Delilah,* Saint-Saëns's piece of academic rubbish. Delilah,
too, is a killer, since she cuts off Samson's hair—which reduces
him to servitude, causes his eyes to be put out and, stripping him
of his strength, is tantamount to a castration. I also heard her sing
arias from *Tosca,* that other piece of rubbish by Puccini, adapted
from Victorien Sardou's drama in which the singer Floria Tosca
(my aunt's role) stabs Scarpia, the chief of police, after which the
latter manages to have her lover, the painter Mario Cavaradossi,
shot. One thing about this last work that seemed clever to me
was that my aunt, a singer, should actually play the part of a
singer.

THE FLYING DUTCHMAN

HERE there was no murderess involved. Senta, the heroine of Wagner's drama, is in love with the Flying Dutchman and deliberately drowns herself to raise the curse of eternal wandering that weighs on the condemned mariner.

Tante Lise had no success in the role of the young suicide, probably because a role of such devoted sweetness did not suit her temperament. But with what majesty the Dutchman himself was cloaked for me, that magnificent figure who must sail the seas for centuries, pursued by his punishment!

Emaciated and bearded like a new Jokanaan, wearing a sailor's waterproof, a long spectral cape, and high buccaneer boots, the Dutchman who cannot die and drags his ghastly, green-faced crew along with him is indeed the most hallucinatory hero for whose salvation a girl can sacrifice herself.

I suspect that this fantastic figure—too great for me to have even dared hope to resemble—counts for something in the romantic idea I have always had of salvation by love, and in the magical attraction exerted upon me—until I actually made a slow and remote journey—by the notion of vagrancy, the impossibility of stopping, settling and, more precisely, of becoming established in that particular point of space materially and emotionally *given* instead of wandering from sea to sea.

When—not more than two years ago—I traveled through Africa, I thought many times of the "cursed specter" with whom I was tempted—whenever circumstances lent themselves to a certain mythical exaltation—to identify myself somewhat.

NARCISSUS

THE only utterly tame role which Tante Lise performed, to my knowledge, is that of the good countrywoman Toinette in *Le Chemineau,* the farrago of nonsense by the composer Xavier

Leroux (who had long gypsy mustaches like my Alsatian school-master) and the "poet" Jean Richepin. However, I happened to see it performed around the same time as a lyric drama entitled *La Vendetta* (of which I now remember nothing except the suggestive title) in which she also figured.

This latter performance was completed by a ballet entitled *Narkiss,* which was considered indecent and caused a scandal at the time. It was a Ballet Russe retelling of the myth of Narcissus, based on a tale by Jean Lorrain. I remember vast processions of virtually naked men with bulging pectorals, and the Egyptian Prince Narkiss, a handsome boy wearing nothing but gold rice powder and a jockstrap. I also remember a man in a similar costume only green, and, above all, a North African woman naked to the waist, so that I could stare my fill at her nipples and navel, which I had never been able to do with any other woman, save in a fragmentary and stealthy manner.

I greatly regretted at the time (and, above all, greatly fretted, for this suppression led me to think that there was something incomprehensible and sinister about the matter) that one scene had been cut; especially since it was described in the program. In the last scene, we were to see the gilded Prince Narkiss lured by the dancer with the naked breasts (a kind of lascivious witch, half demon and half dragonfly), to a pestilential pool where—seduced by his own reflection—he would immerse himself up to the shoulders; at the moment when only his head is still out of the water, the woman would pluck it off and carry it away, as if it had been a flower.

Aside from the fact that I was disturbed by this scenario which everything combined to make me regard as *evil,* with all the charm that such an idea involved, I overheard two tall, graceful men in evening clothes exchange in the lobby the following comment on the actor who played Narcissus: "He's pretty, but not well enough built." From their manner, I realize now that these men were simply homosexuals. At the time, not even knowing what homosexuality was, I baptized them "aesthetes." But I was long haunted by the notion that there was something *perverse* about them, and I became aware of the existence of an entire world apart, of a forbidden domain, taboo and "erotic," as was proved to me by this scene which for some mysterious reason had been censored.

I was also profoundly disturbed by the idea that there existed "sexless" men, "castrated" men analogous (it seemed to me) to the eunuchs who figured among the characters in the ballet. Combined with the sweet, gentle but somewhat overpowering image of Tante Lise, this caused me to envisage love as something menacing and fatal, in which one risked losing one's life, just as Holofernes lost his in the course of an all too gallant supper.

RECAPITULATING and comparing Tante Lise's roles, I notice —not without a certain amused astonishment—that this beautiful, kindly, placid woman, for all her bourgeois and conventional character, appeared to my child's eyes as nothing less than a man-eater.

Rather than the sword-swallower, I regret that it was not she who had married my uncle the acrobat.

V

The Head of Holofernes

Then, lured on by a spell, when we had supposed it was
only by the beauty of the place, we came to a peristyle
at the entrance to the palace; but no sooner had we
reached it when the marble upon which we were walking, solid in appearance, divided and dissolved beneath
our feet; an unexpected fall precipitated us under a
moving wheel armed with terrible knives which in the
twinkling of an eye had cut our bodies into pieces, and
what was most surprising about this was that death did
not follow such a strange dissolution.

Borne on by their own weight, the portions of our
bodies fell into a deep ditch, and there mingled with
the multitude of heaped-up limbs. Our heads rolled like
balls. This extraordinary movement having utterly
dazed what little reason so supernatural an adventure
had left to me, I opened my eyes only after some time
had passed, and saw that my head was set on the steps
opposite and facing eight hundred other heads of both
sexes, of every age and color. These heads had retained
the movement of their eyes and tongue, and above all of
the jaws so that they yawned almost continually.

(Cazotte, quoted by Gérard de Nerval
in *Les Illuminés*)

O NE OF THE earliest memories I have is of the following
scene: I am seven or eight years old and at school; on
the same bench with me is a girl in a gray velvet dress,
with long curly blond hair; we are studying a lesson together in
the same *Sacred History* text that is set on the big black wood
table. I still see quite clearly the illustration we were looking at:
it represented Abraham's sacrifice; above a kneeling child with
clasped hands and exposed throat hovers the patriarch's arm,
wielding an enormous knife, and the old man raises his eyes to
heaven, seeking the approval of the wicked God to whom he is
sacrificing his son.

This print—a wretched illustration from one of the pages of a
children's book—left an indelible impression upon me, and vari-

ous other recollections gravitate around it. First of all, other legends, read in history or mythology textbooks, such as the story of Prometheus whose liver was devoured by a vulture, or the anecdote of the Spartan child who had stolen a fox, hidden it under his tunic, and although the creature cruelly bit his chest, said nothing, preferring to suffer a thousand torments rather than reveal his theft. Then dreams, the first ones I can recall: once, I am in a woods, apparently in the middle of a clearing; around me everything is green and the grass is strewn with daisies and poppies; suddenly a wolf appears, its jaws gaping, and throws itself upon me—with its pointed ears, its gleaming eyes, and its big wet pink tongue dangling between white teeth—and devours me. Another time it is a carriage horse that eats me, and it is still painful for me to recollect the rickety old yellow-and-black carriage driven by a sordid coachman in a white leather cap. Then there are other images from the same *Sacred History:* the Red Sea swallowing up Pharaoh's army; the tortures inflicted on the Maccabees by Antiochus, King of Syria; Judas Maccabeus's brother being crushed to death under the elephant he has just stabbed; Moses and the burning bush.

These various recollections are associated for me with a threat my older brother once made to remove my appendix with a corkscrew, as well as with the threat of a schoolmate, with whom I had fought, to have his father bash in my skull with an ax; they were also connected with a disagreeable impression made upon me by an accident that had occurred to a boy of my own age, who had given himself a deep cut in the wrist and wore an enormous bandage, under whose whiteness I imagined the bloody wrist almost completely severed, the hand virtually detached from the forearm. Then come, in broader and vaguer waves, recollections of various events, such as the sounds of a street fight heard one evening when my parents and I were leaving my uncle's house, which was in a bad neighborhood; or the dreadful shrieks of a woman crushed under the Métro, at one of the most sinister stations of the elevated lines to the outer boulevards.

Completely dominated by these childhood fears, my life seems analogous to that of a race perpetually victimized by superstitious terrors and in the clutch of dark and cruel mysteries. Man is a wolf to man, and animals are good only to eat or be eaten. Perhaps this panic fashion of seeing the world is connected with my various recollections relating to *wounded men*.

THROAT CUT

AT THE age of five or six, I was the victim of an assault. I mean that I endured an operation on my throat to remove certain growths; the operation took place in a very brutal manner, without my being anesthetized. My parents had first made the mistake of taking me to the surgeon without telling me where we were going. If my recollections are correct, I believed we were on the way to the circus; I was therefore far from anticipating the nasty trick about to be played on me by our old family doctor, who assisted the surgeon, as well as by the latter himself. The occasion went off, point for point, like a play that had been rehearsed, and I had the feeling that I had been lured into a hideous ambush. Matters proceeded as follows: leaving my parents in the waiting room, the old doctor led me into another room where the surgeon was waiting for me, wearing a huge black beard and a white gown (such, at least, is the image I have kept of the ogre); I saw various sharp instruments and must have looked frightened, for the old doctor took me on his lap and said to reassure me: "Come here, *mon petit coco*! Now we're going to play kitchen." From this moment on I can remember nothing except the sudden assault of the surgeon, who plunged some kind of a sharp instrument into my throat, the pain that I felt, and the scream—like that of a slaughtered animal—that I uttered. My mother, who heard me from the next room, was terrified.

On the way home in the carriage, I did not speak a word; the shock had been so violent that for twenty-four hours it was impossible to get a word out of me; my mother, completely disoriented, wondered if I had become a mute. All I can remember about the period immediately following the operation is the carriage ride, my parents' vain attempts to make me speak, and then, back at the house, my mother holding me in her arms in front of the living-room fireplace, the sherbets she had me swallow, the blood I spat up at each mouthful and which mingled with the raspberry color of the sherbets.

This recollection is, I believe, the most painful of all my childhood memories. Not only did I not understand why I had been hurt, but I had the notion of a deception, a trap, a terrible perfidy on the part of the adults who had been kind to me only to be able to make a fierce assault upon my person. My whole image of life has been scarred by the incident: the world, full of traps, is nothing but a huge prison or an operating theater; I am on earth only to become a specimen for doctors, cannon fodder, food for worms; like the fallacious promise to take me to the circus or to play kitchen, everything nice that can happen to me meanwhile is only a deceit, a way of sugaring the pill in order to lure me more securely to the slaughterhouse where, sooner or later, I must be taken.

PENIS INFLAMED

A FEW months (or years) later, I suffered from a disease which was, I believe, the infection known as balanitis and which, according to the Littré medical dictionary, consists of an "inflammation of the mucous membrane covering the glans of the penis." It was treated by local applications of a potassium permanganate solution; I distinctly recall my pleasure in observing the solution, whose brilliant violet color varied in intensity according to the degree of its concentration. I felt a slight itching sensation, neither pleasant nor disagreeable, but I was most alarmed by the sight of my swollen member. Since I suffered, moreover, from a congenital tendency to phimosis (which was later a great source of shame for me when I compared my genitals with those of other boys), there was some discussion at this period of having me circumcised, but the operation proved to be unnecessary.

I am incapable of distinguishing this morbid turgescence from my earliest erections, and I believe that initially the erection frightened me because I took it for another outbreak of the disease. Of course my affliction had also given me some pleasure, on account of the hypersensitivity which it afforded, but I knew that it must be something bad and abnormal, since I was being treated for it.

The first conscious manifestations of my erotic life therefore occur under the sign of the *inauspicious,* and the disease from which I then suffered must count for a good deal in my early apprehensions of physical love and my fear of venereal disease. For a long time I believed, for instance, that a man's loss of virginity necessarily involved pain and bloodshed, as is true of women; given my physical structure, it seemed to me that in my case these would be worse than for others. On the other hand, my elder brother, purportedly warning me about the dangers that threaten every adolescent, one day told me about a certain little boy who, because he had slept with his "whore of a housemaid" at the age of twelve or thirteen, had (my brother said) become a chronic invalid, a proper punishment for his precocious love life. This was enough to make coitus seem to me an act not only culpable if one gave oneself up to it too soon, but eminently dangerous.

HURT FOOT, BITTEN BUTTOCK, CUT HEAD

THE suburban locale I have referred to earlier as the arena of certain of my childhood's most crucial episodes is connected in my mind with two or three memories of injury.

Like many children my age at the time, I was at the height of my heroic and Napoleonic fantasies. I had been taken to visit the palace of Versailles and what struck me most, aside from the famous "Capture of the Smalah of Abd-el-Kader," was a famous painting of "Napoleon Wounded at Ratisbon." Often, in my games, I reconstructed the scene: wearing a paper *bicorne* and straddling a wheeled, long-haired beast that was supposed to be a goat but which I insisted was a donkey named "Mirliflore," I stretched one shoeless foot toward the ground (as I had seen Napoleon do in the painting, from the height of his mount) as if, mastering the pain by merely puckering my lip into a disdainful pout, I calmly waited for my wound to be dressed. I acted out this scene in the garden, on the pebbly path that surrounded the lawn, and as I bared my foot quite close to the gravel I felt the same enigmatic and disturbing sensation that I had experienced, in virtually the same place and at the same period, at the sight of children climbing trees barefoot.

That same disdainful pout—which my mother called my "lip" and which seemed to me to be a supremely virile expression—I also assumed when I put on the toreador costume inherited from my other brother, who had worn it on the occasion of a masquerade; hooded cape carelessly thrown over one shoulder, I paraded about with a pearl-handled sword and gravely performed my part as a *torero* wrapped in his cape.

One day a cousin whose parents lived in the villa next door to ours was bitten by a dog. One detail made me shudder: I was told that the bite had been so deep "a piece of buttock had remained in the child's underwear." I cannot think of this cousin —who was subsequently killed in the war—without remembering what he was like when the incident occurred: a big, well-built, heavy-set boy whose parents adored him because he represented, from a certain point of view, the ideal of beauty and health, and whose chubby calves were the admiration of almost everyone in the family, except for my mother who said he was a "big softy" and thought her sons "more delicate."

THE villa we rented during the summer had no running water, and every day we had to line up at the pump, armed with

buckets, kettles, and other receptacles. One day when I was coming back with my sister and the cleaning woman, we were the in-
voluntary witnesses of an accident. A young butcher-boy bicy-
cling down a slope at top speed took the turn badly or skidded:
he ran smack into the arch of the railway bridge and fell over
backward, his head cut open, his arms outstretched in a cross (?),
his twisted bicycle collapsed beside him. My sister immediately
ran to him, washed his bleeding forehead with the water we were
carrying, and tended him until he came to. "Like a saint," the
cleaning woman said later, marveling at my sister's devotion.

This scene made a tremendous impression upon me: the sud-
denness of the accident, the bicycle leaping up as if to climb the
embankment, then falling back, the unconscious boy in his sky-
blue and white butcher-boy's uniform, and the red blood flowing down his face, and my sister bending tenderly over him to
dress the wound. It seemed to me that, as the cleaning woman
said, my sister was indeed a "saint" and that by caring for this
injured boy she had done something quite beyond her age, something very moral yet perhaps rather daring too, which immediately raised her from the category *jeune fille* to the status of
woman.

NIGHTMARES

WHEN I was not yet considered old enough to be taken to the
opera, I was allowed to attend matinees organized by a little
"Cercle Artistique" to which my father belonged, serving as
treasurer, I believe. The sessions took place either at the town
hall of our arrondissement or—for the more formal ones—in the
great hall of the Trocadéro. A funereal place: the huge, dusty,
icy nave, the great organ pipes falling in stupid stalagmites behind the stage, the echo that made the place detestable from an
acoustical point of view, the smell of old people and boxwood
wreaths, the municipal decorations of the boxholders with their
official epaulets and beribboned lapels, the whole county-fair

aspect, a respectable celebration somewhere between a kermis and a choral society. I have been back there several times: at twelve and thirteen for prize distributions (reported the same evening in *Le Temps,* which afforded my parents and me the satisfaction of seeing my name in the newspaper), and then much later on for an Isadora Duncan concert (I found her, of course, sublime), Chaplin's first visit to Paris, etc. . . . Whether it was for the Cercle Artistique programs, the Lycée Janson-de-Sailly prize-giving, academic dances, or a phlegmatic Charlot in a black suit exhibiting himself next to a rubicund and befeathered Cécile Sorel, this hall with its wretched and official appearance— a combination morgue, license bureau, and auction house—has always made chills run up my spine. My last sight of it was during its demolition: the enormous enclosure strewn with debris, without floor or chairs (so that the steel skeleton was exposed), looked like a parliament after a revolution or an earthquake, an old carcass of a ship or some marine monster; then, when the whole interior had been destroyed and even the cupola had collapsed, it became a Roman ruin, a circus with Moorish windows along its walls and in an adjoining space the statue of La Renommée capsized in a corner like an animal that has just been hit over the head, while the wind flapped mournfully overhead in the torn hangings. Disguised as a crumbling arena, at that moment the Trocadéro theater was really beautiful.

As for the Cercle Artistique, its programs corresponded perfectly to the funereal ambiance of this hall. Among the entertainments, there were two that scared me to death.

First of all, the exhibitions of the Secouristes Français, the society for first aid to victims of street accidents. This organization included among its most eminent members a more or less Polish squireen who presided over the Cercle Artistique, whence the conjunction of the two groups. The demonstrations of assistance to the sick or wounded were generally presented in the following fashion: a man with a cane and a hat walked rapidly out onto the stage; about halfway across, he suddenly collapsed. Two *secouristes* in street clothes with red and blue armbands (the colors of the city of Paris) rushed toward him; in the twinkling of an eye they had picked up the victim and carried him to the wings, employing means that varied according to the case: carrying him under the arms, by means of canes forming a stretcher, or even on two bicycles with a device serving as a litter between them.

The moment this character appeared on the stage, I foresaw his fall (remembering from the preceding sessions what was to happen), and it was the expectation of this collapse that agonized me most. I don't know if my uneasiness then and subsequent impressions of the same order should be traced to a common and very early source (to which might also be related, for instance, my emotion at the sight of those poor children climbing up the trees at the risk of bruising their bare feet or falling), but I have always reacted with the same blend of fear and pity to anything having to do with *fait-divers,* the trivial expression of fatality. I am frightened, for example, by street accidents, especially accidents—or fights—which occur in summer (when the weather is hot and sunny, when people are sweating and women wear light dresses that leave their arms and necks bare) or even on holidays, during vacations or Sundays (when people are coming home from a walk), in short, by events reported as a "bloody Christmas," "a Bastille Day that ended badly," "a tragic swim," or by joys which turn sour (like the childhood laughter that inevitably leads to tears, or the periods of overoptimism whose ineluctable conclusion is a dizzying plunge into depression), anything which figures as a "lightning bolt in a cloudless sky," the spectral appearance at the end of a banquet, the misfortune occurring when everything seemed so calm, like war exploding during a period of prosperity, or the police charging a peaceful crowd at the most unexpected moment.

When I am in the street, I never mingle with any kind of demonstration; the sight of human blood flowing in broad daylight terrifies me.

Writing these lines, I recall one sordid thing recently glimpsed near a hospital past which I was riding in a streetcar: the wounded foot (naked, filthy, its corns gleaming in the sunlight) of a workman whom two of his friends were carrying from the construction yards where an accident had just occurred. I imagined this workman going home, the reflections of his neighbors, the abashed look of his children, his wife's hysterical gestures and exclamations; a day that might have begun so well, and now this terrible accident! Such is life: one day, my wife, too, will look at me with a shocked stare; I'll be suffering from cancer, or I'll be crippled. Nothing to do about it! I'll lose every shred of dignity and courage in the face of the thousand minor miseries which pounce upon the sick and the dead: having to use a bedpan, being unable to control one's sphincter muscles, stinking, liquefying. . . .

If it is a beautiful day, I am filled with anxiety: it's a bad sign that the weather should be so fine, what terrible event is in store? Similarly, if I take any pleasure at all, I calculate my chances of paying for it in the near future, and a hundred times over! for fate is nothing but a usurer.

Aside from these demonstrations of first aid for the victims of accidents, there was another offering almost equally abhorred: a middle-aged and corpulent woman who recited poetry, draped— if I remember correctly—in a classical robe; I can imagine her even wearing a Phrygian cap, a monumental "République." Among the poems she recited, there was one called "The Nightmares," the only one of which I have any recollection at all:

> . . . *At night, when all begins to slumber,*
> *The nightmares come!*

Then followed a description of nightmares, of terrible creatures huddled in the corners like hideous invalids.

Declaiming horrors in a voice as cavernous as possible, her imposing stature magnified by the rigid folds of her gown, this

woman was to me the living personification of the dreaded nightmare I somehow identified with my father's raucous snores I
sometimes heard in the middle of the night, with the sinister
sounds that seemed to me to come from the other side of the
grave and that I now identify with the death rattle of his last
hours.

I listened to that woman's deep voice, which itself so resembled a snore, convinced that I would hear it again the moment I fell asleep and that I would have to struggle to keep from
evoking lugubrious visions which, if they did not materialize in
dreams to trouble my sleep, would at least haunt me for hours
before I could relax, panic-stricken, my body rigid and drenched
with sweat.

MY BROTHER MY ENEMY

MY ELDER brother, who was supposed to be talented at drawing, was studying at the School of Decorative Arts. To my other
brother and to me, he was the typical habitué of the Latin Quarter, someone who rubbed elbows with bohemians, was allowed
to sit on café terraces, had the privilege of seeing and even of
talking to naked women, since there were models in the studios
where he worked; furthermore, he was the one who had revealed
to us the existence of the "portel."

My other brother and I were generally in league against this
elder brother, not only for reasons of age, but because our tastes
and characters were more alike. We had the same mystical idea
of love—which we conceived of only as a *unique love*, the goal
and substance of a whole lifetime—and professed the same disgust for those frivolous creatures represented by the "libertines."
Our education had contributed greatly to the formation of this
state of mind; I remember, for instance, what my parents said
about the plays of Henri Bataille, regarded as fundamentally
immoral, in any case "not for *jeunes filles*," so that we could
almost divide the latter into two categories: those whose parents
took them to plays by Henri Bataille, i.e., "modern" *jeune filles*

(a distinctly pejorative epithet), and those whose parents did not.

Without quite belonging to the "libertine" category—for the poor boy was too phlegmatic by temperament and too restricted in funds and clothes for it to occur to us to assign him to a caste we presumed to be so brilliant in these respects—our elder brother was nonetheless suspected by us of impulses in that direction on account of his artist's profession, his associations, and particularly because of his contact with models. Powerfully built and of an optimistic temperament, he was greedy, playful, and quick-tempered. Aside from his threatened operation on my appendix with a corkscrew (an operation he himself had undergone, but under normal conditions), he had once spoken of "making me eat button soup." At this period, one of the soups served most frequently at home was a kind of bouillon with noodle dough cut in various shapes—stars, numbers, letters of the alphabet—floating in it; I envisioned mother-of-pearl buttons instead of these pieces of dough, and my revulsion was so great that even today I cannot see a shirt button without imagining it in my mouth and verging on nausea. Another torment consisted, somewhat later, of locking me in his bedroom and staring me in the eyes while reciting poems in a tremulous voice, until I begged for mercy or burst into tears. I add that having learned from my own lips that I masturbated regularly (a confidence I made to him, as to my other brother, for naïve purposes of propaganda), he had said he would tell our father on me; I doubt that he actually did so, but I remember my confusion, that evening when our father came home from the Bourse—wearing the flat-brimmed top hat he affected—and when I believed each glance he gave me during the evening was a suspicious scrutiny to discover the telltale stigmata on my face.

As for his rages, I remember having seen him, when all three of us were still very young, throw a heavy metal candelabrum at my other brother's head because he thought he had cheated at cards; this candelabrum, one branch of which remained twisted, still decorates the mantelpiece of my mother's living room. Another time, for some reason, he fought with my father, rolling over and over on the living-room carpet; it was during dinner, and I can still remember a bottle being brandished, to my mother's terror, by one combatant or the other. My parents were troubled by these outbursts; they kept anticipating the possible consequences: blows, injuries, even murder, some day, when my older brother "saw red"; striking a superior officer when he was doing his military service, which would involve a court-martial. . . . Of course, as is almost always the case with such parental fears, these turned out to be perfectly groundless: today my elder brother is a well-behaved bourgeois, the father of a whole tribe of children.

I always obscurely hated this elder brother, originally because of his strength and today because of his vulgarity. To me he is the perfect example of the philistine; not that he is altogether insensitive, for he has always had—rather like my father—certain artistic and literary tastes (it was, for instance, in his books that I first read poems by Baudelaire and Verlaine); not that he is absolutely without humanity (he refused to serve in the 1914–1918 war except as a stretcher bearer); but on account of his comfortable, easygoing manner, sentimental without passion, deistic without mysticism, respectable without fanaticism. It is difficult for me to imagine what he might have done except for being the father of some half-dozen children. I cannot endure his pipe, his heavy face with its huge mustache, and the impression he gives of complete security.

It would be difficult for me today to grasp what it was that made my other brother and me categorize him even partially as a "libertine" if it were not for the simple fact that he was older than we and that he knew about brothels—in short, that he was already an *initiate* whereas we were still only children. A good deal of our antagonism must have been based on this circumstance, and no doubt it was primarily a question of a rebellion against the prerogatives of the most powerful.

When we were on good terms with him, my brother took us more than once on expeditions with him: I remember, one summer at an English seaside resort, a walk when we almost vanished

into a quicksand, having taken a short cut across a bay;—and one
Easter vacation, climbing up Mont Saint-Michel by its steepest
slope;—and early in the war, at Biarritz, the sickening ascent of
a rocky crag almost entirely surrounded by waves (I wanted to
give up halfway there, but my brother sarcastically made me
promise to go back alone, so I decided it would be better to continue);—near Biarritz, too, the wild descent (running, flinging
ourselves from tree to tree, from peak to peak) of a hill it had
taken us a good hour to climb. At that same English resort—filled
on Sundays with a crowd pouring out of charabancs and so
drunk in the evening that they danced in huge gangs, ladies and
gentlemen exchanging hats—my brother, jostling me, had shoved
me into some barbed wire (and my calves were badly cut) following some argument over the hotel chambermaid with whom he
was infatuated, and afterward—which shamed me—we had
passed a pretty girl in a beret who had actually made me blush
to the tips of my toes.

Two accidents, as far as I can remember, occurred to this elder
brother—one when I was so young that I don't know if I really
remember it or if I am reconstructing the scene according to
what I've been told about it, the other when I must have been
about ten.

One evening when our sister was putting us to bed, my
brother, standing on his bed and using the mattress as a spring-
board, improvised a kind of wild dance to tease her. This took
place just when my sister was giving him the chamber pot. A
leap more violent than the rest and my brother, losing his bal-
ance, collapsed right onto the chamber pot which crashed to the
floor in a thousand pieces. He stood up, his head drenched with
urine. Touching him in the half darkness, my sister felt his damp
head and, taking this for blood, assumed he had seriously hurt
himself. Her fear was all the greater in that my brother, apparently, did nothing to undeceive her; perhaps he had taken this
opportunity for a good piece of teasing, perhaps the violence of
the shock had somewhat dazed him.

Later, when he was studying at the School of Decorative Arts,

my brother came home in a strange state one day: one of his
hands was bandaged, his face was red, he seemed strangely over-
excited and kept singing:

> *They're in the vines, the sparrows!*
> *They're in the vines!*

tearing around the dining-room table without our being able to
stop him. My mother could not imagine what was the matter
with him, and it was only after a certain time that he was able to
explain himself clearly enough to give my mother the key to the
situation: one of his workshop colleagues—a boy from our neighborhood who used to attend the same gymnasium if not the same
school we did, who passed in my mother's eyes for an "original"
if not a lunatic, and who, according to my brother, had once tried
to "violate" a young student of the workshop (an operation
whose mechanism I was quite vague about at the time, not knowing what sodomy was)—one of his classmates, as I was saying, who
was wasting time tossing his knife into the tabletop, had accidentally stabbed my brother's hand which had been in the
blade's trajectory; the victim had drunk the entire contents of a
small bottle of rum as a kind of cordial, and this had made him
completely drunk—the first time such a thing had ever happened
to him, and even then requiring the excuse of a nearly pierced
palm. The wound was not serious, but according to the pharmacist who had dressed it, my brother was extraordinarily lucky his
hand had not been paralyzed.

MY BROTHER MY FRIEND

I SHOULD never be finished if I tried to enumerate all the stories
of injuries with which my childhood is strewn, wounds that occurred sometimes to me, sometimes to one or the other of my
brothers: a barley-sugar stick sucked to a dagger point and run
into a knee because someone fell while running, an eye black-

ened by a medicine ball, a deep cut made by a pocketknife that had managed to slice off a fingertip instead of a pencil point, a bump on the forehead usually treated with arnica or the application of something cold like a coin—all the various and minor accidents which make your parents or elders say, if you haven't been good: "It's God who's punishing you!"

I have never been very wild, still less pugnacious, in general rather timid, sulky, and inclined to complain. There was little or no need to tell me: "Don't pet strange dogs!" or "Don't play with matches!" or "Look up and down before you cross the street!" I was much too afraid to be bitten, burned, or run over. Today, I am scarcely more assertive, and the only exercise I enjoy is a walk (a long stroll in the country or a dark promenade through the streets of Paris, when one feels like hiding). The anecdotes I am telling here do not, moreover, represent anything crucial or exceptional for me; I offer them simply because they come to mind apropos of this idea of *injury*—a wound inflicted on a man with whom I identify myself (if it is not myself who is involved) or who touches me very closely, is linked to me—in sympathy or animosity, positively or negatively—by a special relationship. The three that follow may have importance insofar as they characterize certain of my ways of reacting. The first two relate to my second brother and to myself, the last to myself alone, and I regard it as a kind of pendant to the operation which affected me so strongly when I was four or five; perhaps the reason for this is that I am concerned in both incidents, and that in the second I showed myself to be brave, which seemed to me a kind of revenge for the first, in which I remember only my pathetic terror.

I have referred to the understanding that prevailed between my second brother and me. Of analogous temperaments in more than one respect (fundamental melancholy, a tendency to mysticism, a dramatic sense of life, etc. . . .) we agreed on many points; and, from this distance, I am astonished at such an understanding when I measure the difference (perhaps, after all, more apparent than real?) of the roads each of us has subsequently taken. We had a common morality (a certain Puritanism) and a common mythology, woven out of all kinds of stories —sometimes supposedly factual narrative, sometimes fiction of a purely fantastic order (which we adored inventing). We held our council every evening in the bathroom (my brother sitting on the stool—the appanage of the elder—and I opposite, on a vulgar pot) and told each other long stories—generally a kind of interminable epic serial with animal characters—each continuing the story in turn, alternating day by day.

Among the "true" stories my brother told me, there is one which has figured more than the others as a legend I believed thoroughly and whose hero was aureoled for me with an almost mystical halo. At a period when we were greatly interested in sports—especially in races, since the Auteuil Hippodrome was near our house—my brother described how he had won the Grand Prix de Paris with his hoop. He drew a detailed plan of the race track: the starting point (near the municipal greenhouses, a place where we often were taken to play); the dense crowd in a double row; the other competitors, boys almost the same age as my brother; the head start he had at the beginning, leading all his adversaries; the impeccable style in which he had continued until almost the end of the course; his disastrous fall —slashing his knee badly—when he had practically won the race; the heroic manner in which he got to his feet, mastering his pain; the desperate effort he had made to catch up with his adversaries; the agonizing battle he had waged, passing them one by one until his final victory, after which he had collapsed, overwhelmed with fatigue, among wild acclaim from the endless crowd of spectators electrified by his courage.

This narrative, which my brother often recited, virtually without variations, and in which I maintained an absolute belief, conferred upon him, in my eyes, that almost superhuman greatness which children attribute to historical personages whose high deeds are recounted to them: Charlemagne, Bayard, Turenne, or Napoleon. Even more than my brother's sporting prowess, it was the lesson in courage that I admired, the endurance he had shown, the stoicism with which he had defied his wound, trying his best right up to the end, despite his exhaustion and suffering, and yielding to physical weakness only after having emerged from the ordeal, like a hero who agrees to abandon the scene of a disaster only after everyone else has been saved.

I note that this admiration—this sensitivity, above all, to *stoicism*—already contained the element which today still characterizes my ideal of courage: a courage that is not *aggressive* but *passive*, that consists of neither extraordinary actions nor deeds of military valor but, for instance, of the *sang-froid* with which one behaves when faced with some hideous danger or, better still, of one's capacity for resisting some dreadful torture.

IT IS again my second brother who figures in the following adventure, of which a critical phase occurred in a hotel at Le Havre, on the Quai de Southampton. I don't know whether I should consider this incident—actually quite a trivial one—the sign of some obscure predestination, but I have always loved Le Havre, other harbor cities, and especially river ports such as Nantes. I am not particularly sensitive to the lure of the sea, I have never been able to learn how to swim, I am a land animal and not at all a water creature; but I adore, for instance, being on a steamer and I am interested in everything which in any way relates to navigation.

Several of my friends come from Le Havre or from Nantes. Among my most happy memories are those of visits, generally very brief, which I happened to make to such places—notably one of several days spent in Le Havre in 1924, accompanied by a friend even more experienced in traveling than I and who had just settled himself in Paris after spending several years in an Eastern European capital where he taught philosophy. I again saw the Quai de Southampton with its swarms of people, its restaurants, its little bars, its Hôtel de l'Amirauté which, about twelve years before, had been the scene of the adventure in question, and its Rue des Galions which I then discovered, a flaming trench containing a double row of Edens guarded by matrons wrapped in woolen shawls, sitting on stools and chanting invitations. Of all the places at which my friend and I paused as we walked along, the one which still attracts me most is the now vanished "Silver Dollar," an English bar—or claiming to be English—which was located between a church and a police station. Here there were two French barmaids—blonde sisters with snaky hips and pointed breasts, who danced with the customers, played zanzibar and poker, and poured drinks while wriggling like *haute couture* models. They were helped by a servant-girl, who must have been milking cows just the day before or perhaps the week before that. Among the display of bottles above the bar sat two huge, ogling English dolls. On an ancient upright piano, in the room adjoining the bar, a white-haired, wretchedly dressed old man, his dignified face only slightly the worse for alcoholic wear, delicately strummed waltzes, mazurkas, and polkas in between operetta tunes, national anthems, and patriotic marches; occasionally he stood up and approached one of the rare customers, collecting his tips in a tiny ashtray that was doubtless in proportion to his take. Now and then one of the sisters laughed loudly, one hand on her hip, her little belly stuck out; the little servant-girl sat without saying a word—her forehead wrinkled, but apparently from thought rather than irritation—and left her stool only for the comings and goings of her work or to listen to the old musician at closer range, leaning on the piano and singing under her breath, as though to accompany him. The intimacy of the place was violated only by half-drunk American sailors who immediately took over the instrument and pounded out fox trots whose notes spattered the ceiling like many-colored drinks or else accumulated, dripping foam, like strong beer. Someone told me that one of the two sisters got married and that the other has grown fat and sad.

A less exact recollection, but a more suitably nautical one, is that of my first return from England, when I was about twelve. Shortly after the ship had left Dover, a "dry storm" came up, with long rolls of thunder and an almost uninterrupted series of lightning flashes at all points of the horizon; it was extremely dark, and the effect was all the more striking since there was not a breath of wind and despite the stormy light the sea remained absolutely calm. I have often told people—and I am quite incapable of saying today if it was altogether false—that at the height of the storm St. Elmo's fire broke out on top of one of the masts.

Another sea memory is my departure from Marseilles, after I was married, when I first tried to escape by flight what was gnawing at my vitals. I was sailing to Cairo, to meet the same friend with whom I had wandered through the old neighborhood of Le Havre. As the steamer slowly pulled away, I saw the strip of water appear, then widen between the hull and the quay. A moment of heartrending fulfillment, impossible to recover once this virginity of the first sailing is lost. In it, you take the measure of things, the distance that separates you from them, and are thereby able, for once, to take your own measure as well.

Something similar happened to me during the course of the most recent trip I made to Le Havre, last Pentecost. I had spent the night in various bars, dance halls, and night clubs, not to mention the sinister dives in the Rue des Galions; everything seemed a little dead compared to what it had been several years before; not many people in the streets, nobody drunk, no player pianos. Still, I had that impression of profound humanity and grandeur that I believe one experiences in any house of prostitution provided it is poor and its routines sufficiently simple. This was on Pentecost Monday, which perhaps explains the relative calm of all these places. "Church celebrations aren't brothel celebrations," sententiously declared one little whore to whom I had remarked in some astonishment that there were so few people in the establishment where she was employed. After many conversations in many places, I had managed to drink enough so that the next morning I was terribly thirsty for a deep breath of sea air to refresh my heart and restore order to the ideas dancing in my head. So I took a walk beyond Sainte-Adresse, along the cliffs. About fifty yards above the sea there is a point of high ground from which I overlooked a little creek, where I suddenly faced myself more intensely than any time since my departure from Marseilles. Out at sea, a clanging buoy danced on the waves, and I heard the harsh music of its bell. And on the shore, moving from rock to rock with insect precaution, were two boys in raincoats and berets, accompanied by a middle-aged bourgeois woman who must have been their mother, all of them apparently on vacation, and out for a stroll, like myself. One of them, equipped with a mineralogical hammer, occasionally chipped off a sample piece of rock from the cliff. I was still imbued with my hangover from the night before, and it suddenly seemed to me that the solitary buoy I heard clanging now was none other than the little prostitute to whom I had talked and who had appeared to be so humble, so gentle, so "well-bred."

It seemed scandalous that despite the lugubrious voice of this bell which sounded as though it was calling for help (the little whore had told us that she had been confined in her tiny cell for fourteen months) someone could divert himself by mineralog-ical research, lingering along the beach, hammer in hand. And to a certain degree, I identified myself with him, involved as I am—by my incapacity to ignore certain material needs such as comfort—in scientific work which I consider paltry, while at the heart of the world, as out to sea, beyond this bay, there was some-thing so passionate, raving, crying all alone, asking only to be heard, asking you to have enough courage to dedicate yourself to it utterly. Walking back, I thought for a moment of returning to the brothel to sleep with the little prostitute. I did not do so, and no doubt I was wrong, even if there had been only the most unromantic consequences, such as a vulgar venereal disease, after some commonplace and commercial embrace.

Here I am far from what I intended to tell as I began the

penultimate section of a chapter devoted to events of my life that
relate to the theme of the "injured man." Even as I write, the
plan I had devised escapes me, and one might say that the more I
look into myself the more confused everything I see becomes,
the themes I originally hoped to distinguish proving inconse-
quential and arbitrary, as if such classification was ultimately no
more than an abstract guideline, or merely a simple procedure
of aesthetic composition.

The "recollection of Le Havre," involving my second brother,
is mingled in any case with that of my first Channel crossing. It
was during the Easter vacation. Our parents had taken us to
Trouville (apparently the suitable place for children our age at
the time), and on this trip we had invented a fiction that had become almost a myth. At this period, we were both fascinated by
races and often pretended we were jockeys boarding with their
trainer; since we were minutely informed as to the performances
of the chief stars of the turf, we had no difficulty identifying ourselves with one celebrity or another; thus, for several years, my
brother was none other than René Sauval; for some time, I in-
carnated Nash Turner; later, I was George Mitchell because of
the surname's resemblance to my own first name. But during the
trip in question, I may have been the French jockey Parfrement.
An astonishing glamour attached to these names, and such iden-
tifications had apparently no other purpose than to make us
powerful by incorporating into ourselves the spirit of those persons we admired. We might just as well have identified ourselves
with the saints of the catechism.

From Trouville, our parents had taken us by the paddle boat
La Touque on an excursion to Le Havre, from which we were
to return by the same means of transportation at the end of the
day. They had not counted on the fog which suddenly closed in
and prevented the boat from leaving, so that we had to remain at
Le Havre and, without any kind of baggage, seek asylum for the
night at the Hôtel de l'Amirauté. My brothers and I, naturally,
were delighted by a contretemps which turned an already attrac-

tive excursion into a kind of adventure. More familiar than we with the banality of such an incident even in its unforeseen qualities, our parents did not share our delight, particularly since it had begun to rain and they knew the three of us together would be too turbulent to be cooped up in a hotel room. The game my second brother and I played proceeded as follows: the two jockeys, with their trainer and his wife, were on their way to a race that was to be run the following day; events were complicated by an adultery, for it was understood that Parfrement, i.e., myself, had been fortunate on this journey and become the lover of the trainer's wife, who was none other than our mother, of course.

My parents remained in a corner of the room, evidently quite out of sorts, obliged as they were to spend this night in their daytime clothes, without toothbrush, comb, or any toilet articles. My father must have been wearing his eternal top hat (when we returned the next day, the fog having lifted, the sea was rather high and I can still see my father flattened by seasickness, his top hat over his eyes, huddled in a corner). Were we perhaps all camped in one room because the hotel was full (hence the story of the adultery)? In any case our parents were not in very good humor, and this circumstance increased our own nervousness. We ran about the room in all directions, unable to sit still and wanting at any price to see what was happening outside. My second brother leaned against the window to look out into the street; the pane gave way and fell with a tremendous crash onto the sidewalk, then full of people, for the rain must have stopped. At the sound, our mother dashed to the window, but she thought she had heard cries and hesitated for a long time before leaning out, afraid some passer-by had been injured by the splinters of glass and not daring to determine whether or not this was actually the case. Finally she leaned out, glanced down onto the quay, saw that no blood had been shed and that the crowd continued to come and go as before. She came back to the middle of the room, still trembling, but reassured. It was only then that we were scolded. The incident, moreover, cut short our game, for our mother's alarm—and all the possibilities of punishment it suggested (the police coming to arrest us, or the hotel manager) —had terrified us into silence. The night was passed one way or another; I had plenty of time to ponder my little adultery with the trainer's wife, and the next day on the boat, I was very proud to see my father flattened by seasickness which I myself did not suffer from or at least gave no evidence of, except perhaps for a certain pallor.

I have spoken of passion, of a prostitute of inimitable sweetness, of St. Elmo's fire, of a bell clanging over a calm sea. Why is it that all that delirious ardor increasingly escapes me and that, like my mother resting a fearful hand on the windowsill of the Hôtel de l'Amirauté, I scarcely dare glance even briefly out the window, for fear of finding only a little blood on the quay?

STITCHES

OF THE last episode to be related here, I myself was the hero, and I still bear the scar of it under my left eyebrow. On certain days (particularly when the weather is hot) it is redder and more visible, seemingly recent, so that I am occasionally asked what injury I have just suffered.

I was twelve years old, attending that school run by a priest, where I had made my first Communion; and the incident occurred in the school courtyard, during a recreation period. Running at top speed—in some game or gymnastic contest—I collided with one of my schoolmates coming in the opposite direction, and was dashed against the wall so violently that I split the flesh open to the bone just beneath my left eyebrow. I remained kneeling—or on all fours—on the gravel, head down, bleeding heavily. Apparently I lost consciousness, but I have no recollection of this, and actually supposed, before I was told I had fainted, that I had remained conscious throughout the incident. Since the wall was on my right and my head had been injured on the left side, I did not realize that I must have pivoted around before falling to the position in which I was making these stupefied reflections. At first I thought that the mere encounter of my forehead with that of my fellow pupil had cut my face open; it was only later that I learned that I had torn my flesh against a rough place on the wall, or against a nail stuck on this wall. I felt my blood flowing; I wasn't suffering from the slightest pain, but so violent had the shock been that it seemed as if my wound must be enormous, and that I had been disfigured. The first thing that occurred to me was: "How can I ever make love?" I don't think that I was in love with any particular girl at the time; it was merely a matter of the future, which I envisaged from a purely emotional angle and which seemed to me, because of the wound that was certainly hideous, irremediably spoiled. "How can I ever make love to anybody?" I asked myself, and the question filled me, rising from my heart to my head, and I would certainly have collapsed under its weight if by its very formulation I had not sensed that I had acceded to a certain exalting tragic level which afforded me both the pride of having to play a part and the necessary strength to play it properly. The trousers of my Norfolk suit were bloodstained, and there must also have been blood on the flannel-lined high-button leggings—the ones which, a year or two later, my *lycée* schoolmates baptized "grand-father's boots"—so long a required article of my winter ward-robe, to my great mortification.

I was picked up and carried to the kitchen, where the woman in charge, sickened by the sight of blood and twice sighing *"hélas!"* washed my wound before taking me to the pharmacist. The latter (who had a big beard and a stiff leg, having been run over by a bus) dressed my wound and made me drink a little glass of alcohol as a restorative. I did not hesitate to ask for a second, delighted by the unexpected treat and convinced, no doubt, that this was one of the elementary requirements of the role fate had assigned me. I was escorted home and my horrified mother took me to our own doctor. He sutured my wound with three metal

clasps, telling my mother that she should consider herself lucky
I got off so cheaply, for if the wound had extended as far as the
temple (and it would have taken only a few millimeters to do so),
it might have been fatal. The idea of having been so close to
death filled me with pride, of course. About two weeks later,
when the doctor removed the stitches, using a tiny penknife as
a lever, I did not flinch, though the pain made my eyes fill with
sudden tears. This stoicism caused the doctor to congratulate my
mother, which made me all the prouder, for it is not often that I
have had occasion to manifest my courage this way.

Thus occurred—shortly after I had learned from a school
friend the true nature of sexual intercourse—an event which did
not disfigure me but from which I have retained a noticeable
scar. It won me a brief popularity at school, and in particular a
private delight at having seen death at close range, at being the
survivor who has luckily escaped alive from a disaster.

MY MANNER of presenting things may bring forth the charge of
a certain arbitrariness in the choice of facts I am recording. I
have already described the attraction exerted upon me by everything that appeared in a tragic light, and I shall not discuss it
again; a double current, of mingled anguish and desire, like
everything that attracts and at the same time repels me with regard to Judith.

Admitting that there is something arbitrary about it, I do not
see what the bias of such a choice can reveal if not, precisely, this
predilection indicating the exceptionally disturbing value which
sanguinary episodes have for me, and figures on a platform, wearing cothurni, or stuffed into grotesque masks.

FITFULLY, from question to question, from mystery to mystery (discovering first that children were made in their mother's
womb, then that their father was no banal Saint Joseph limiting
himself to winning bread for them but played an indispensable
part in their creation, and finally that the famous act consisted—

at first it seemed to me an absurd joke—in the conjunction of the urinary organs), I had little by little acquired a theoretic knowledge of love. Obsessed by ghosts, I now had to acquire, and at what cost, its practical knowledge as well.

VI

Lucrece and Judith

I am traveling by foot in a mountainous country which is supposed to be rather dangerous. Having walked for a long time, I reach Delphi (which I have actually visited). Behind the ruins of the temple, countless stretches of desert extend as far as the eye can see. At the end of each expanse lies a chain of mountains. Behind each chain, another stretch of desert, also bounded by a chain of mountains masking a third desert, and so on. It is the aggregate of these delimited wastelands which constitutes the true desert—the desert in itself. But between the debris of column fragments and these empty spaces lies a deep ravine which I cannot cross. Its walls—so steep they seem absolutely vertical—appear to be animated by a constant oscillating movement. The air in the crevasse, because of the uniformly repeated movement of these flat walls, echoes with a sinister noise, like a volcanic rumble or the crackling of a thunderbolt. But actually the walls are motionless, and it is the wind caught in this abyss which is the cause of this sound. Shortly after this truth has been realized, bearded men—probably officiating priests of the temple—hurl enormous blocks of marble into the abyss. At the bottom, these blocks break into a thousand pieces, making a tremendous racket.

(A dream, 1928)

AMONG the legendary narratives which I most loved as a child and which have not ceased to amaze me, figure the stories of the Round Table which I first read not in their complete form, but in little illustrated booklets for children, extreme condensations that were perhaps all the more striking for having been expurgated, because all the accessory details were removed and nothing remained except the very essence of the myths.

I have always loved what is childish, primitive, innocent. When I am what rigorists call "good" I aspire to evil, because I need a certain evil in order to entertain myself; when I am what is conventionally called "evil," I feel a vague nostalgia, as if what most people understand by "good" were really a kind of maternal breast from which I might suck a restorative milk. My whole life consists of these oscillations: calm, I am bored to death and long for almost any distraction, but as soon as any real upheaval occurs in my existence, I lose my footing, hesitate, evade, and generally abandon. . . . I am incapable, in any case, of acting without reticence and without remorse. I never surrender to anything without a mental reservation to correct myself, and if I fall back on my own thoughts it is never without regret for a surrender I crave. As an adult, I preserve a constant longing for ideal friendship and platonic love beside what some will regard as ignoble immersions in vileness and vice. As a child, I was enthralled by those fabulous adventures filled with wizards, knights, and impossibly chaste damsels, at the same time that the confusions of puberty stirred within me.

One story that impressed me more than all the rest and that even as I copy out these lines holds me under its enigmatic spell, is the legend of the disappearance of King Arthur. It is not known if he ever really died. After his sword, which he had thrown into the lake, had appeared three times, brandished by the hand of some submarine creature, the fairies carried him off to an island, as he lay on his death bed in a boat. There was also the episode of Merlin, lost in the forest of Broceliande where Vivian, his mistress, held him prisoner by the very charms he himself had taught her. Often, as I reflected on this story, it seemed to me a kind of image of my own life—the life of a man who gorged himself on pessimism, believing he would find in it the means to a dazzling and meteoric existence, loving his own despair until the day he realized—too late—that he could no longer emerge from it, and that he had thus fallen into the trap of his own enchantments.

From this chaos of armor, of hennins and throats of lunar whiteness in which my imagination reveled, there has emerged the concept of the *sorceress,* of Woman as I both desired and feared her, the enchantress containing all sweetness, but also concealing all danger, like the courtesan (a word that begins with "courtly" to end with "partisan," which—at the still recent period when I attached an oracular value to this kind of play on words—would once have seemed to me an unshakable argument in support of my theory) or like that female character which might symbolically combine my Lucrece and my Judith: Cleopatra, Queen of Egypt.

ONE of the last things I think of if I pronounce the name of Cleopatra is Pascal's remark about her nose, and I don't even know if it was supposed to have been longer or shorter for the face of the world to have been notably changed thereby. I detest such aphorisms, which sound as if they were saying so much and which explain nothing. This may not take us far, but it is in any case certain that if I say "Cleopatra," I think first of the asp hidden in a basket of figs (like most people, I hate snakes), then of the lions to which she threw her lovers.

I think also of the word "alabaster," whose purity Cleopatra shares; then I evoke images of porticoes, of columns past which stroll Alexandrian philosophers—old tramps in rags—who interfere in my memory with what I know of modern Alexandria: the steaming heat (I still think with disgust of my clothes covered with a humidity worse than the moisture of my own body); the motley of the native quarter near the harbor; the astonishment with which I discovered there a "Bar Normand" run by two whores who were no doubt Norman and who must have been, before the avatars that had brought them there, robust farm girls; the Arab families camped on deck of the *S. S. Boulak* on which I sailed to Greece with a box of wafers and a bottle of white wine for provisions. With these memories of Alexandria, I combine other images of my stay in Cairo: the pyramids of Giza, like enormous heaps of coal on a pier; the blue square carved out of the sky by the walls of the inner gardens of mosques; the taverns with nickel-plated ultramodern machines

producing ice-cold drinks that will corrode your stomach if you
are not careful; a certain strolling peddler in the native quarter,
a skinny man wearing a graying goatee and a turban, who poured
out tamarind syrup in a long jet, holding his urn very high above
the glass, with an inimitable elegance; the Scottish officers in
plaid trousers or in evening dress (evening slippers and tuxedos
over the plaid kilt); the vagabonds with their bronze skin and
long nightshirts; the bourgeois in red fezzes, light suits, with non-
chalant fly-whisks, walking importantly or sitting at tables on
café terraces; the lane of bougainvillea trees on the island of
Gezira, so rich in blooms that when the sun shone you walked
through it as though through a red fog; the hot sandy wind
which on certain days burned the inside of my nostrils (this
makes me think, at this moment, of the pottery I tried to make as
a child, heating wet sand over a candle and producing a vague
odor of burned cake, and using for molds such ordinary house-
hold objects as egg cups); the Ezbekieh neighborhood where the
black prostitutes are shut up in a sort of cage—raised floor opening on the street through a wide bay window, the dark arm reach-
ing out through the bars to grab you; the Arab singers in their
décolleté dresses, breasts overflowing with medals like wrestlers;
the figures with heads of birds of prey and broad, widespread
wings that you see in museums or on the walls of cemeteries;
the paintings on the sarcophagi of the Roman period (delicate
women's faces, fresh and carefully made up); the Egyptian
women in blue or black gravediggers' veils, with their dirty bare
feet or flirtatious high-heeled hideous slippers, when they are
somewhat wealthier; the unbelievably chaste life I led in this
city, having no sexual relations with any human being, but
sometimes satisfying myself on the laths of the floor.

It was after the troubled years when she ordered the men she
had used thrown to the wild beasts (I do not believe this detail
figures in Plutarch or in any other historian, but that does not
matter, for the essential thing is this double role of an authori-
tarian sovereign and a woman of loose morals), after the "match-

less life" with Mark Antony, the pearls dissolved in wine, the foundation of the club of the Inseparables in Death and all the other whims which must have sprung from her unbridled imagination—it was after these that Cleopatra, unable to seduce the victorious Octavius, caused herself to be bitten on the breast by an asp, preferring death to the servitude which threatened her.

Examining the circumstances in which Cleopatra, Queen of Egypt, ended her life, I am struck by the contact of these two elements: on the one hand the murderous serpent, the male symbol par excellence—on the other the figs beneath which it was concealed, the common image of the female organ. Without attempting to find anything here but a coincidence, I cannot help noting with what exactitude this meeting of symbols corresponds to what for me is the profound meaning of suicide: to become at the same time *oneself and the other,* male and female, subject and object, killed and killer—the only possibility of communion with oneself. If I think of absolute love—that conjunction not of two beings (or of a being and the world) but rather of two great words—it seems to me that it cannot be achieved save by means of an expiation, like that of Prometheus punished for having stolen fire. A punishment one inflicts on oneself in order to have the right to love oneself to excess—this, in the last analysis, is the meaning of suicide.

And if we now consider Cleopatra not only as a woman of an abandoned life (a woman scoffing at her lovers), but as a creature eliminating herself from the world, we realize that she sums up these two aspects of the eternal feminine, my Lucrece and my Judith, obverse and reverse of the same medal.

We may wonder, seeing Cranach's double painting, if it is not analogous links which have connected the two heroines in the artist's mind, Lucrece the chaste, and Judith the patriot prostitute, so that he decided to represent them in one pair of figures. One might also suspect that their two apparently distinct gestures were at bottom identical, and that both were supremely concerned to cleanse in blood the taint of an erotic act, the one expiating by her suicide the shame of having been violated (and perhaps of having enjoyed that violation), the other expiating by murder the shame of having prostituted herself to her victim. So that it would not be out of mere caprice, but by virtue of profound analogies, that Cranach painted the two as pendants, both similarly naked and desirable, at one in that complete absence of moral hierarchy which is the necessary concomitant of nakedness, and shown on the verge of committing particularly arousing actions:

the first, Lucrece, pressing to the center of her white chest, between two marvelously hard, round breasts (whose nipples seem as rigid as the stones decorating a gorget or cuirass at the same place), the narrow blade of a dagger whose tip is already beaded, like the most intimate gift appearing at the end of the male member, with a few drops of blood, and about to annihilate the effect of the rape she has suffered by a similar gesture: one that will thrust into a warm sheath of flesh, and for a bloody death, the weapon at its maximum degree of stiffness, like the rapist's inexorable virility when it enters by force the orifice already gaping between her thighs, the gentle pink wound that soon after returned the libation in full measure, just as the wound— deeper, wickeder too, but perhaps even more intoxicating—made by the dagger will release, from Lucrece's very heart as she faints or fails, a torrent of blood;

the second, Judith, in her right hand a sword naked as herself, its point piercing the ground close to her slender toes and its firm broad blade having just severed Holofernes' head, which hangs, sinister trophy, from the heroine's left hand, fingers and hair mingled in hideous union—Judith, wearing a necklace as heavy as a convict's chain, whose coldness around her voluptuous neck recalls that of the sword close to her feet—Judith, placid and already seeming to ignore the bearded ball she holds like a phallic glans she could have sundered merely by pressing her legs together when Holofernes' floodgates opened; or which, an ogress at the height of her madness, she might have cut from the powerful member of the drunken (and perhaps vomiting) man with a sudden snap of her teeth.

And thus—even more naked than they are in Cranach, where only a transparent veil swathes their loins identically—they stand before one another, the two great classical nudes, equal angels of good and evil, situated, by the blood that spatters them, on the same plane of murder where all mediocrity is effaced. But the pale and unhappy Lucrece, the absurdly dedicated slave of conjugal morality (yet to what purpose since it was her chastity that lured Tarquin to her), is nonetheless eclipsed by the insolent image of Judith as she must have appeared, emerging from Holofernes' tent (in which the treacherous creature had sought protection), her sharp nails dyed by murder like those of a woman lacquering hers red in the fashion of the twentieth century, her clothes rumpled, covered with sweat and dust and hastily pulled back on—in the greatest disorder—revealing here and there her flesh still sticky with ejaculations and blood. Like Holofernes with his head cut off, I imagine myself sprawling at the feet of this idol.

In my memory lie—like miscellaneous objects (anchors, chains, shirts, pencils, paper) in the ship chandler's shop where the navigators come to provision their ships—a certain number of events, many of which may be considered as ridiculous or base; but the very "vileness" that may be attached to almost all these events and the extreme fear and repugnance I suffer in evoking them result, even when they do not have an immediately terrifying woman as a heroine, in making Judiths of those women who have been involved in them (less, in this case, by their own attitude than by the defeated attitude I adopted toward them). Thus I see several Judiths of flesh and blood, however approximate, rise before me:

THE little girl—her hair parted down the middle, with black combs and a dutiful expression despite her lusty appearance and her malicious glances—with whom I went to school and who, as many children enjoy doing, rubbed one wrist with the palm of the other hand for a long time, making me smell the skin thus rubbed and telling me: "That's what death smells like";

a blonde (peroxided) widow, heavily made up, wearing black and white veils, silk stockings, and a big bouquet of violets, across from whom I found myself sitting in the streetcar, and whose tired eyes, red mouth, and legs I stared at in order to memorize them for my solitary nocturnal festivals;

the real or false creatures for whom I wept in my bed, bitterly ruminating in solitude and despair at never finding a woman adequate to my love, stirring up these smarting images until I burst into sobs, great gasps into which I plunged as into a tide of caresses;

the eminently inaccessible actresses, such as Sarah Bernhardt, who for a while was one of the favorite themes of my masturbation fantasies;

the barmaid with whom I was in love at fifteen, because she was a Lesbian and had a rasping voice, and because I had heard her groan during a toothache—a trickster who purely and simply fleeced me, not even sleeping with me and running away with the money which, like a fool, I had given her, a fact which unimaginably humiliated me—the same girl, too, with whom my father had once surprised me, which had caused me to be ashamed beyond all expression;

the girl—a customer in another bar—who bit my lips until they bled and kicked me in the face, one day when she was drunk, to show me how lithe she was;

the girl in lace underwear and black silk stockings with whom, being a virgin, I found myself in bed after a night of wild drinking, but whom I could not touch because I began to vomit a pool of red wine all over the sheets;

the girl no longer young but still pretty whom I met in a whorehouse while I was still a virgin, and with whom I locked myself into a bedroom with elaborate furnishings but whom I could not manage to possess because, despite her kindness and the wet kisses with which she maternally covered my forehead, I

was too upset, and unable to move my arms and legs out of
anxiety;

the friend with blue eyes and an English name whom I "truly"
loved, but with whom the same phenomenon occurred the first
time we went to bed together, so great were my apprehensions
that my inexperience would be exposed—a woman whom I was
later to suspect of deceiving me (or of wanting to deceive me)
with a young girl, and of being generally curious about love for
members of her own sex, a treason perhaps still worse than sleeping with another man, for this is indeed a question of *another*
love, against which it is impossible to do anything;

the whore encountered one night in an American bar, where
I was drinking with an older, homosexual friend of mine—a
typical "beautiful bitch" type, tall and dark, who aroused me
by pressing her powerful thighs against me when we were dancing, but who (after a violent scene during which she insulted
my friend who—for some reason I no longer remember—had
scratched her) terrified me by her bestiality;—after this incident
I had taken my friend back to his house, dead drunk and suffering from nausea, and then slept with him after having humiliated my mouth and his own in a reciprocal frenzy;

the cold, arrogant American woman who during the course
of a night's drinking, in which I participated with the same
friend, calmly informed me that she had committed a murder, a
confidence which I now regard rather skeptically;

the submissive whore who, after endless descriptions of intimate details and torments, showed us the knife scars on her buttocks, and whom I never slept with but often think of when I
read newspaper accounts of street fights or stories of women murdered and hacked to pieces;

the girl who had become the mistress of my accomplice in the
three preceding adventures; when I first saw her I was royally
drunk and attempted to make love on an enormous canopied
bed with a very young whore, gentle and pure as some Lucrece;
I savagely bit her, enraged by my drunken impotence, while my
friend and his companion (who possessed Judith's bitter smile

and disarming eyes) sat together in a huge armchair and seemed
to enjoy my shame, with another whore standing beside them
and vainly trying to persuade them to join me, as they laughed
hysterically; I did all this to accept an unspoken challenge
(which this magnificent Judith, without even knowing it, had
flung at me with all the brilliance of her Gorgon's eyes, after a
long dialogue in which I had proudly assumed the pedestal of
amorality, speaking as an unbeliever and a desperate man); and
I believed that after such an encounter I had literally nothing
to hide;

the whore with whom I went on a four-day drunk, a fine girl,
but vulgar and not at all pretty, with legs (on which she showed
me the black-and-blue marks one client had inflicted) that were
shapely but too thin for her enormous breasts, whose nipples she
concealed with her hands as if they were infirmities, because
their excessive diameter made them look like wine stains, like
burns, like crushed raspberries, or even like the hideous scars
a razor might have produced; I desired her because I was lonely,
because it was she who, after a long period of depression, happened to be under my hand; I desired her—although she was the
opposite of the kind of woman I prefer—and I measured my vileness at the same time, perhaps, that I was fascinated by the fact
that she humiliated me utterly by the way she behaved everywhere we went, getting me nearly murdered by all sorts of people, and between alcohol and insomnia almost annihilating me;

the whore with the old, withered face, a pathetic, provincial
creature with a delicate body, fine skin, and subtly perfumed
thighs and throat, who assumed the grand airs of a chic demi-
mondaine, showing off her elegant clothes and manners, but
who, corrupted by drugs, her sleep broken by groans, sudden
gestures, and nightmares, would suddenly shriek aloud, completely unconscious, in a voice that had turned completely raucous: "Aren't you through yet, you old bitch, do you have to
wake me up to stick another man into me?"

the others whom I shall list in their proper time and place;

and lastly, the ones who do nothing, the ones I dare not even
speak to when I meet them, but who cut my throat with nothing
but their Medusa eyes.

FOR a woman, to me, is always Medusa or the Raft of the Medusa.
By this I mean that if her gaze does not freeze up my blood, then
everything must ensue as if we compensated for that by tearing
each other apart.

Apparently I was an obedient and good-natured child, but I
have retained virtually no memory of this, and if it were not for
the explicit evidence of my mother and my sister, I would today
refuse to believe it. I know that very early in my life, I had a
predilection for tears, as well as for a certain degree of histrionics.
It would be almost impossible for me to say at what moments,
even when I was very young, I was really *natural,* at what moments I was playing a part not, in truth, out of deliberate hypocrisy (for, quite often, I was my own dupe) but from an instinctive
need to magnify myself in the eyes of others or in my own. My
family regarded sensitivity as a virtue characteristic of its members; my brothers and I were praised as "delicate natures," "sensitive boys." Hence I adored dissolving in tears or even indulg-
ing in tricks that were likely to accentuate this sensitivity, such
as deliberately burying myself at the bottom of my bed, so that
someone would tenderly put me back where I belonged, and
sympathize with me for sleeping so restlessly. When my second
brother—who was really talented—played some long sonata or
other classical piece on his violin, I worked myself up to the
point of tears, in order to acquire a reputation as a precocious
music lover, and because I enjoyed those tears with a positive
voluptuousness. One night early in the war, my sister—who had
been sent with me to Biarritz—found me in tears, my face buried
in my pillow; she had no difficulty making me confess the reason:
my love, though I was scarcely more than thirteen, for a woman
over thirty; all the same, in this particular case, I believe my distress was not entirely counterfeit.

As a general rule, each time that I had sobbed enough, I felt a sense of calm, of relaxation, and fell asleep in a kind of euphoria, as if everything had been explained and as if (though such words are scarcely adequate) *my tears had regenerated me.*

Later, when these impulses, which were after all relatively authentic, combined with a certain knowledge of literature, I gorged myself on verses like Verlaine's on Woman:

> *Douce, pensive et brune et jamais étonnée*
> *Et qui parfois vous baise au front, comme un enfant!*
>
> *(Pensive, sweet and dark, forever surprised,*
> *Who sometimes gives your brow a childish kiss.)*

or like Poe's passage on the lost beloved, image of an impossible love:

> *For the rare and radiant maiden whom the angels name Lenore—*
> *Nameless here for evermore!*

Among novels which touched me deeply during the torments of puberty figures Zola's *Nana*, which I loved not so much for its corrupt atmosphere, the filth of its dressing rooms, and stale whiffs of the boudoir, as for the episode of Georges Hugon, an adolescent runaway whom the kindly whore plays with in her bed as if he were a dog or a little child.

In a red-lined notebook bound in gray buckram, where, around the age of fourteen, I wrote sententious poems and maxims, I find these lines which, of course, seem quite foolish and wretched to me today, but which still correspond to what—scarcely daring to admit it to myself—I childishly persist in desiring:

> Oh! to live with a beloved woman, tender as a mistress, sweet as a mother, who would share my pains and my joys, driving away the harsh suffering that gnaws at my heart, warding off the melancholy boredom of my mind with one glance of her clear eyes, or

with a single long kiss from her cool mouth! Yes, I would be understood at last. I would weep in a woman's arms, weep without fearing mockery, weep assured of being consoled!

I believed, like so many boys of my own age, that I was more
misunderstood than anyone else in the world, and I dreamed of
entirely ethereal mistresses over whom I wept, knowing I would
never find them, or of maternal women in whom I could take
comfort, forgetting on their breast my longing for the inaccessible, and with whom, above all, I would be allowed to weep.

Since then I have lost this faculty of tears, and I am tempted
to regard this as a punishment for having too complacently abandoned myself to these fits of self-indulgent sentimentality. There
are many occasions when I should like to be able to sob, but
every day I realize with a little more disgust that nothing but
physical pain can wring tears from me now.

So if there are women who attract me to the degree that they
elude or else paralyze and terrify me—like Judith—there are also
sweet Lucreces who are my consoling sisters, the only ones with
whom I do not feel constrained. And if, dreaming of Judith, I
can conquer only Lucrece, I experience so extreme a sensation
of weakness that I am mortally humiliated. Only one way, then,
remains by which I can reinstate myself in this tragic atmosphere
which I have chickenheartedly avoided; this will be, in order to
love Lucrece better, to make her into a martyr. The result of this
is that, in practical terms, if the woman I live with does not in-
spire a holy *terror* (I use the word "holy" because the notion of
the sacred is definitely operative here), I tend to replace this absent terror by *pity;* which comes down to saying, in more precise terms, that I always tend to make myself pity the woman in
question by artificial means, with the help of a kind of moral
laceration which I introduce into everyday life, trying to transform it somewhat by these repeated pangs into a "Raft of the
Medusa" on which a handful of starved survivors mourn and
devour each other.

Thus I find that this exaltation, of a very particular order, linked to what terrorizes me in the sexual realm, recurs to a certain degree in pity, so that (like Judith and Lucrece regarded purely from the angle of bloodshed) these two poles again become virtually identical. For if I examine the nature of this pity with sufficient exactitude, I perceive that the intoxicating confusion I suffer from it derives above all from the *remorse* attached to it because it is I myself who have behaved in a cowardly fashion, and cruelly enough to occasion such pity. Hence this delectable remorse indirectly leads me back to terror, under the circumstances: the superstitious fear of punishment. But arranging matters so that when I betray I do so only in pain —that is, on a level where I myself am also the victim—I manage, in relation to the other person, to regard myself as quits, and thereby experience a certain alleviation. Thus by the play of contradictory forces, everything is always subject to a double movement.

I cannot express myself clearly here, not out of mere cowardice upon exposing one of the things I am most ashamed of, but because ultimately the two notions of terror and pity remain ambiguous for me. Exactly as—on a virtually identical scale: tenderness and agony mingled—my feelings remain ambiguous when I recollect certain childhood memories: the white rams with golden horns in a crèche someone had given me (perhaps I loved them because I already had the vague notion that sheep are doomed to the slaughterhouse); or myself in a blue-and-white-checked apron, moaning: "I'm bored!" with my head pressed against the cool windowpane.

When modern investigators invoke the unconscious, refer to Oedipus, castration, guilt, and narcissism, I do not think this advances us greatly as to the essentials of the problem (which remains, I believe, linked to the problem of death, to the apprehension of nothingness, and therefore concerns metaphysics). I can, however, cite one anecdote which shows the profound importance which I instinctively attach to the relationship between fear and beauty, an anecdote dating back to a period of

my life when I had no conscious interest in any such connection.
Some may consider this anecdote significant:

IN 1920 or 1921, when I first became enthusiastic about modern
poetry, my hysterical resentment of my father, to whom I had
read a poem by Apollinaire (the one in *Alcools* called "1909")
and who had characterized as incomprehensible and absurd the
two last and admirable lines:

> *Cette femme était si belle*
> *Qu'elle me faisait peur.*

> *(That woman was so lovely*
> *She terrified me.)*

VII

The Loves of Holofernes

I bear in my hands the disguise by which I conceal my life. A web of meaningless events, I dye it with the magic of my point of view. A fly crushed between my fingers proves my sadism to me. A glass of alcohol drained in one gulp raises me to the level of Dostoevski's great drunkards. And when I'm drunk, I'll make my confession, omitting, of course, to say how, in order to ignore the banality of my life, I make myself examine it only through the lenses of the sublime. I am neither more nor less pure than anyone else, but I want to see myself as pure; I prefer that to seeing myself as *impure,* for to achieve a certain pitch of impurity one must expend too much energy. And I am fundamentally lazy.

In every respect, I am like the *petit bourgeois* who gives himself the illusion of being Sardanapalus by a visit to the brothel.

First I wanted to play the part of Rolla, then that of Hamlet, today that of Gérard de Nerval. Which tomorrow?

I have always chosen masks which did not suit my nasty *petit bourgeois* face, and I have imitated only what was easiest to imitate in my heroes.

I shall never hang myself, nor poison myself, nor be killed in a duel.

How would I dare look at myself if I did not wear either a mask or distorting lenses?

My life is flat, flat, flat. Only my eyes seek cataclysms within it. Actually I fear only two things: death and physical suffering. Toothaches have kept me from sleeping; I can hardly say as much of my moral agonies.

After this discovery, I should indeed commit suicide, but that is the last thing I shall do.

(Entry in a diary, 1924)

I AM THINKING here of one woman in particular, whom I shall refrain from identifying, and of whom I shall say nothing, in fact, except that she was both Lucrece and Judith— Lucrece because I can regard her as having been, in a certain sense, the victim of my wickedness; Judith by all her stigmatized and ravished qualities. I can add that I had immediately attributed a *Racinian* quality to her, and that I am tempted to describe her as Phaedra still more than as Lucrece or Judith.

Our fates coincided only momentarily, but however limited—even sketchy—our relations, this quite recent meeting has revealed me to myself so suddenly and so intensely that I can scarcely continue with this account (so aware am I now of my desperate circumstance) in a state of nakedness that excludes any possibility of creating myths for myself, or those semilegendary poles to which—however ardently one aspires to sincerity—one always refers because they alone permit one to live.

I address this woman here only because she is absent (to whom does one write save to someone absent?). By her very remoteness she mingles with my nostalgia, insinuates herself between me and most of my thoughts. Not, certainly, that she could be a *loved object,* but only a *substance of melancholy,* the image—fortuitous, perhaps, but nonetheless appropriate—of all I lack, i.e., of all that I desire and that inspires me with this desperate need to express myself, to formulate in more or less convincing phrases the always too little I experience, and to fix it on paper. I am imbued with the notion that a Muse is necessarily a dead woman, inaccessible or absent; that the poetic structure—like a cannon, which is only a hole surrounded by steel—can be based only on what one does not have; and that ultimately one can write only to fill a void or at the very least to situate, in relation to the most lucid part of ourselves, the place where this incommensurable abyss yawns within us.

One of the things my "adventure" with this woman has most illuminated for me—and most sadly—is the following. All my friends know it: I am a specialist in confession; yet what impels me—especially with women—to such confidences is timidity. When I am alone with a person whose sex is enough to render her so different from me, my sense of isolation and misery becomes so great that, despairing of finding something to say, incapable too of courting her if I should happen to desire her, I begin—lacking any other subject—to speak of myself. As my phrases flow, the tension rises and I come to the point of establishing, between my partner and myself, a strange dramatic current; for the more my present disturbance agonizes me, the more I speak of myself in an agonized manner, emphasizing my sense of solitude and of separation from the world, until I am ultimately uncertain whether this tragedy I have described corresponds to the permanent reality of my being or is only the imagined expression of that momentary anguish which I suffer as soon as I come into contact with another person and am somehow called upon to speak. With a woman, therefore, I am always in an inferior position; for something decisive to occur between us, it must be *she* who holds out her hand to me; so that the normal role of the conquering male never falls to me, but it is always I who represent, in this duel of two forces, the subjugated element. Furthermore, having actually let myself be mastered and having accepted the occasion, whether or not it conforms to my desires, I experience each time the humiliating sensation of having been satisfied with what is offered, of not having *chosen*. Whence that constant impression of both weakness and betrayal, if it happens that I love and that I am loved.

It was on the occasion of this adventure, too—because of the upheaval provoked in me by this woman, whom I ultimately found more pretentious than touching and grew virtually to detest—that I became able to perceive the mechanism of my constant oscillation between disgust and nostalgia. Detesting myself to the point of virtually wanting to die (while trembling before the slightest threatening gesture on the part of the world); loving what I did not have (even if it was worse than what I had); always wanting to be elsewhere and to attach myself to things and people in their most individual, alien, disturbing aspects and then immediately to withdraw; scorning the involvement which is ultimately reduced to no more than a certain taste for the picturesque, a dilettante's attraction to the exotic, to unknown countries, alien ideas, women with whom I have not slept, either because (with deceptive disdain) I found the grapes too green, or because I chose such objects of desire for their very inaccessibility (which excuses everything, justifies any inertia, since of course there is no argument against the inaccessible)—all this was to conceal from myself that I am afraid of life, which is the truth to be avoided to the very last, since it is harsh and hardly ennobling.

Aside from certain encounters of this kind—and their number is so limited that I am scarcely justified in saying "number" —aside from a few vague erotic friendships, flirtations, or purely venal encounters, I have had only an extremely poor emotional life, its high points consisting of two affairs, one of which—with the woman with the English first name whom I have already mentioned—lasted four years, while the other—my marriage—began nearly ten years ago.

KAY

KAY (for that is the name I shall give her), when I knew her, was in the process of being divorced. It is she who was my initiatrix. This remains inseparable for me from the time when I passionately loved dancing, all things English, and night life; that is, shortly after the war, in that memorable period of "surprise parties" which I suspect will not be forgotten by those who lived through it.

During the years immediately following November 11, 1918, nationalities were sufficiently confused and class barriers sufficiently lowered—at least with regard to the upper middle class—for most parties given by young people to be strange mixtures, where scions of the best families mixed with the dregs of the dance halls. There was a great deal of drinking, a great deal of flirting, and often more than just that—all with the astonishing sense of freedom caused by the mere fact of being a guest of unknown hosts, in the company of a crowd of people who also did not know each other and a considerable portion of whom were not even invited.

At this kind of party, damages were frequent, as were thefts.
Unlucky were the pianos in which, as a joke or out of simple
negligence, one tossed one's unextinguished match or cigarette
butt, or which one baptized with champagne. Woe to the glasses,
carpets, dishes, and on occasion even jewels! A Jewish banker's
wife was robbed during one such "surprise party" given in her
own house by her daughter's friends; after the pseudo-invaders
departed, the honest materfamilias missed a number of items
from her jewel case and discovered on her sheets traces that left
no doubt as to the use to which the conjugal bed had been put.

One gang of boys and girls had a reputation as spongers: they
were on the lookout for every party they could find, and as soon
as they heard that one of these little celebrations was taking
place, they rushed to it; they were not at all interested in the
other participants, danced only with each other and—having
brought nothing, or virtually nothing, in the way of food or
drink—swept the buffet clean in a twinkling, and then went elsewhere; they became so notorious that when they appeared the
friends of the hosts took it on themselves to organize a kind of
cordon sanitaire around the bar and the buffet table.

About a year before the end of the war, jazz had appeared, at
first very different from what it has since become. The orchestra had no brass in it, but only, except for piano and percussion,
stringed instruments: banjos and bass fiddle, which strummed
out the rhythm; furthermore each performance was dominated
almost from beginning to end by the deafening drums. It is a
long way from the implacably obsessive cadences of that period
to even the harshest performances one hears today; the quality
was undoubtedly more mediocre, certainly coarser, and there
was much less invention, but I think I can say, without danger
of my judgment being imputed to the blunting of my senses
(that is, in the last analysis, to the fact that I am now more than
fifteen years older), that jazz was then played with a frenzy that
makes us regret—whatever the undeniable improvement and
perfection they represent—most contemporary performances,

however "artistic" and controlled, save in the very rare cases when the baroque element is given free and intoxicating rein.

In the period of great license that followed the hostilities, jazz was a sign of allegiance, an orgiastic tribute to the colors of the moment. It functioned magically, and its means of influence can be compared to a kind of possession. It was the element that gave these celebrations their true meaning: a *religious* meaning, with communion by dance, latent or manifest eroticism, and drinks, the most effective means of bridging the gap that separates individuals from each other at any kind of gathering. Swept along by violent bursts of topical energy, jazz still had enough of a "dying civilization" about it, of humanity blindly submitting to The Machine, to express quite completely the state of mind of at least some of that generation: a more or less conscious demoralization born of the war, a naïve fascination with the comfort and the latest inventions of progress, a predilection for a contemporary setting whose inanity we nonetheless vaguely anticipated, an abandonment to the animal joy of experiencing the influence of a modern rhythm, an underlying aspiration to a new life in which more room would be made for the impassioned frankness we inarticulately longed for. In jazz, too, came the first public appearances of *Negroes*, the manifestation and the myth of black Edens which were to lead me to Africa and, beyond Africa, to ethnography.

Under this vibrant sign of jazz—whose frivolity masked a secret nostalgia—occurred my union with Kay, the first woman whom I authentically "knew."

In the course of these parties, these walks on the Avenue du Bois, these various social circumstances, I happened to meet a great number of young girls (French, English, Scandinavian, Greek, South American), and consequently enjoyed a number of opportunities for flirting; but I took virtually no advantage of my occasions, first out of timidity, and also because of a vague romanticism, rather Platonic and "blue flower," whose deeper roots I did not at the time suspect. I had passed my *baccalauréat* somehow, toward the end of the war; I was at the age when it is proper to choose what we call a "career," but I was not tempted by anything. When I was younger, my father had dreamed of sending me to the École Polytechnique. Though a short time later, under the influence of a friend I shall have occasion to speak of, I began studying chemistry, I professed the greatest disdain for all exact sciences, refusing to prepare for any degree whatsoever, reading little and doing virtually nothing. Only one profession impressed me, or rather only one label: that of *export and import,* for I imagined one merely had to send around the world typewritten letters itemizing brass ingots, bales of cotton, or cases of whiskey in order to make a great deal of money, and quite elegantly, given the Anglo-Saxon nature of the trade. I had, moreover, the example of a boy I knew, whom I admired for his way of dressing and his friends in fashionable bars, and who had succeeded in making a nice profit out of the liquidation of the American army stockpiles after the war. Actually I did not intend to do a thing, living in the simple expectation of some emotional adventure that would transfigure my existence, releasing me from my profound boredom which was enlivened by no vocational impulse whatever.

Toward the end of this period—agitated on the surface, but already pregnant with all the ennui that was sure to rise to that surface as soon as the first waves had abated—I began spending all my nights out, my inseparable companions being a half-British former classmate, a tall, bony fellow threatened early by tuberculosis, whom I had happened to meet one evening, and a girl a few years older than we were who was slightly lame, rather rich, and studying something somewhere. Our association was based on our love of dancing and also on a predilection for a certain kind of purity, a contempt for sexual interests, which we regarded as vulgar and base, and a severe judgment of life from which we excluded everything except a certain kind of emotional relationship which would also be desperately chaste, our strange three-way amorous friendship serving as a model. We were virtually inseparable. We would generally meet in the morning; a great part of the day was spent wandering about Paris, eating ices or going to dance halls; at night, we went to the "surprise parties" or else to a dancing club frequented by, among other people, the gang of spongers I mentioned earlier. This was the period when people wore very narrow-cuffed trousers and pointed shoes in order to look American; my friend and I worshiped this fashion, and one of our most intense preoccupations was to shake our shoulders in just the right way when we danced the shimmy.

At night, we wandered along the Avenue du Bois or sat on benches and chattered away for hours. Our student friend said she was in love with a rich man, a relative of my ex-classmate's whom she wanted to marry: the three of us laid our plans. The girl was not without charm, but lisped slightly and resembled some kind of nocturnal bird because of her way of closing one eye without narrowing or even winking the other. Perhaps for this reason, we called her Owl. In the same way, my friend had received the nickname Pinhead because of the exiguity of his skull in relation to his slender physique and sloping shoulders.

Owl was something of a mythomaniac, hence her delight in secret councils, intrigues, and whatever gave the illusion of a fantastic existence led by only a few privileged individuals. She complained bitterly about her mother, who she claimed was her stepmother, and had even invented a half-sister for herself, a girl prettier than she who daily berated her with sarcastic remarks, opening, for instance, the bathroom door when she happened to be naked and ironically exclaiming the names of various Greek goddesses. "Venus" and "Diana the Huntress" were the epithets this cruel sister apparently attached to her by antiphrasis, in order to ridicule her limp.

The caresses exchanged between this girl and ourselves came to little enough. We spoke a great deal of our ideal friendship, of despair, of chastity; moreover Owl—perhaps only to insist on her lack of carnal attraction to men—claimed she was a Lesbian:

"I can't think of anything more beautiful in the world than a woman's arm," she often used to say.

We steeped ourselves in the melancholy of certain records, supposedly Hawaiian in origin; sometimes we faked a kind of macabre mood that my old schoolmate and I inherited from our *lycée* during the war, when we embellished our themes and notebooks with drawings of skeletons elegantly dressed in civilian clothes or whimsical uniforms. For we all worshiped at the shrine of the rare, the bizarre, and what we called the "eccentric." Pinhead and I, for instance, professed a great admiration for the military valor of a Scottish officer who led a charge by kicking a football into the opposite trench. The night of the Armistice, I myself had been thrilled in a little theater near the boulevards, one of the favorite rendezvous for night revelers, by the following gesture, which seemed to me sublime in its eccentricity: an ultra-chic boy, who had lost an arm toward the beginning of the hostilities, was sitting on the aisle, very drunk, holding his cane, which happened to be the bone of his amputated arm. He would toss it down into the house for the audience to throw back, everyone laughing hysterically. "Eccentricity" seemed a sign by which the elect recognized each other; this could occur on the heroic as well as the everyday level (for instance: lighting one's cigarette from the flame of a gas street lamp, trying to trip people in the urinal by hooking their legs with the head of a cane, playing some ridiculous trick with a maximum of bitter phlegm). Above all, it was the badge of a confraternity.

I don't know how long this intimacy among the Owl, Pinhead, and myself would have lasted, if a fourth companion had not joined us and entered into the sport, though he was not a virgin and was not at all interested in asceticism. This person was a tall, strong boy, actually something of a brute; he had been mobilized at the very end of the war, which conferred upon him, in relation to Pinhead and me, an elder's privileges. Although there was no overt hostility in our relationship, due to the mere fact of the difference between our physical experience and our manner,

Owl baptized us "Faun" and "Nymph" (myself), which suggests the prestige the newcomer enjoyed in her eyes, without her even realizing it. When I was still at the grammar school I attended before studying at the *lycée,* my friends had given me a feminine nickname: "Gyptis," after a girl who played a crucial part in the foundation of Phocaea, a story which had been the subject of one of our Latin compositions.

Even before my affair with Kay had spoiled everything by betraying our friendship pact, the addition of this new element was a blot on our alliance.

Personally I had no sympathy for the newcomer; his bullying, "lady-killer" manner disgusted me, and I anticipated, between Owl and himself, the kind of explicit sexual event which would destroy the equilibrium of our association. From a more strictly emotional point of view, I was also jealous, sensing between the girl and my two male companions (who, moreover, were friendly with one another outside our little group, and even had certain family links which I have never clearly disentangled) a greater intimacy than with me; as a matter of fact, the three shared certain secrets to which I remained a stranger, concerning Owl's possible marriage, a plot in which Pinhead and our new friend were directly involved.

I was very unhappy, realizing that something had changed in our relation, vaguely foreseeing that all was not going well, but far from suspecting at the time that the actual cause of our breakup would come from me.

Once, without any precise reason but simply in the name of purity, I tried to commit suicide, or rather pretended to try to commit suicide; running away from the other three on the Avenue du Bois, early in the evening, I clutched in my hand a bottle of potassium cyanide Pinhead had brought from the chemical laboratory where he was then studying; of course my friends caught me long before I could have brought the bottle near my lips; the incident ended in tears and reciprocal effusions, but it was enough to maintain an atmosphere.

We made it a point of honor to align ourselves on the side of death, life's very impossibility seeming (as it more or less still seems to me) the great criterion of morality. It was tacitly understood that Pinhead would die of tuberculosis, and Owl already had two suicide attempts to her credit. The first time, at least according to what she had told us, she had swallowed the entire contents of a bottle of laudanum during a party at her mother's house, without succeeding in doing anything worse than giving herself a violent attack of heartburn. Another time, when Pinhead and I had called for her at home, we learned from the maid that she had run out of the house, saying she was going toward the Seine; taking this declaration quite seriously, starved as we were for some tragic event, we immediately dashed after her, but did not even need to catch up with her to keep her from carrying out her sinister design.

Although most of our time was passed quite frivolously, leaning against the walls of some dance hall, and although an observer would have said we were anything but "literary," certain kinds of poetry managed nonetheless to affect us; but of course it had to be the most sentimental, facile, and stupid variety. We were, for instance, wild about some pathetic "bohemians" who ran a vague cabaret with a medieval name. For a whole evening, we gargled their songs; then we sank into depression, envying the "real life" these wretched phonies seemed to lead. Though I cannot be sure, I would not be surprised if my unsuccessful suicide attempt occurred during this phase of our association.

Bar-hopping night and day, drinking quite a lot (especially Pinhead and myself), wearing ourselves out by our conversations, our plots, our secrets, and the complicated nature of our relationships, we soon achieved a state of extreme fatigue which merely accentuated our hypersensitivity.

One night, when we had gone to a dance given by Owl's cousin, Pinhead suddenly fainted between two fox trots or tangoes and had to be taken home. Another morning, walking home after a night of bar-hopping, I began to suffer from all kinds of hallucinations (imaginary silhouettes suddenly turning street

corners just as I reached them, a huge ape bounding over a fence)
which convinced me I was sleepwalking; yet having a taste for
these mirages, I made no attempt to get any rest. Such incidents,
moreover, seemed more comic than anything else, and I recall
that Owl and I once exchanged, half grinning, our impressions
of Pinhead's fainting fits, deciding he was so debilitated that he
would soon be on his deathbed.

We had implicitly agreed that if one of the boys took a mistress (except for the Faun, who was permitted anything, being
situated—in his capacity as a "faun"—or another level) we could
no longer accept him, which meant that the alliance would collapse. Nothing could be more conventional, and doubtlessly we
were merely anticipating what I have had the opportunity of
ascertaining subsequently, which is that love is the enemy of
friendship, that any durable relationship implies a complete
change in perspective—in short, that friendship is really complete only during youth, when couples have not yet formed.
Love attacks at its very foundation that "secret society" spirit by
which friendships, if they are at all profound, are necessarily
dominated.

All my emotional activity therefore found its point of application in this kind of society. I expected no specific kind of love,
conceiving nothing more humanly valid than this friendly complicity (we virtually regarded ourselves as a gang of criminals) in
which I was plunged so deeply. Yet I suffered from an uncon-
fessed languor, verbally rejecting every kind of love and even
calling it impossible, although subterraneously aspiring to a
revelation which would consecrate me as a man and wreak revenge on my past failures.

It would be painful for me to enumerate all my disappointments: the first impulses of love for girls whom I soon renounced, even if they appeared to be willing, either because I
dared say nothing to them, or because I was ashamed, not considering them mature enough and preferring to address myself
to older women who treated me like a child; more precise at-

tempts, such as with the whore in whose company my father had caught me, or my frustrated initiation to the brothel when, without having achieved my goal, I had returned to my companions downstairs announcing that I had been "dishonored"; ridiculous events which served as a kind of fuel to my tearful sentimentality, such as the incident of a prostitute not in a bar who had loaned me ten francs one day and whom I had kissed on the mouth, intoxicated with the notion that I was a pimp, or such as the encounter near the Tabarin—one night when I was wandering around with a gang of other boys—with a woman who had given us the cigarettes we asked for, which moved me to the point of tears; experienced girls whom I courted by words alone (whereas they were expecting more explicit maneuvers) or whom I merely kissed (one, in particular, who was rather fond of me— as I learned later, when she died of tuberculosis—but whose lover I never became because her licentiousness frightened me off); a number of drinks bought for whores who permitted nothing more than a few caresses; debaucheries in hotel rooms, from which I always emerged a virgin; orgies childishly begged for and always botched; abortive flirtations.

The fact remains that (as when I sobbed away in my bed longing for a pair of arms to engulf me) I suffered from a lack so deep I did not even suppose it could ever be satisfied. This fulfillment is what Kay brought me, however, at least during our first days together, and it is possible, after all, that life is worth living if one has had, even for a short period of time, such a sense of plenitude. For my affair with Kay to have occurred at all required, of course, many circumstances which seemed to me quite literally *marvelous*, because my own will did not intervene.

One night, when for once I had gone to bed early, I dreamed of a blissful encounter with a dark woman who resembled, I think, the portrait of the Empress Eugénie in a history book I had read at the time of my first *baccalauréat*. In the state I was in, such a dream was a promising apparition, an angel come to save me. Hence I was not surprised, the next morning, to receive, from a girl I had flirted with a few months before, a chain letter which I was supposed to copy three times and send to three different people. At the beginning of the text, this "chain" was said to originate with an American officer who had returned from the war safe and sound; those who abided by the protocol would receive, nine days later, a "great piece of good luck."

I scrupulously copied the letter three times and sent my versions to three different people, not because I particularly believed in the effectiveness of the ritual, but because I was happy that a friend I had lost sight of had thought of sending it to me, especially at a moment when it almost seemed that, divining my emotional atrophy, she had wanted to help me.

I no longer remember who those three people were; I only know that among them was a girl whom I had known at the same time and in the same circumstances as the girl who had originally sent me the chain letter. She answered me, from the seaside resort where she was staying, by a postcard signed by her first name spelled backward. I solved the riddle quickly enough, and again I was pleased, for it seemed that I was not being forgotten despite my solitude.

Exactly nine days after sending off my three letters, Owl took Pinhead and me to visit one of her friends who lived alone in an attractive apartment, having recently left her husband. Kay was not dark, but blonde and frail, with a touch of arrogance in her face, along with a vivid, intense expression. I learned later that she had been brought up by nuns, and that she had even shown, in early adolescence, some inclination toward mysticism; but none of this appeared in her emancipated manner, except perhaps for that slight look of reserve and dignity in her eyes.

I had then reached the critical point of my exhaustion. I no longer remember what impression Kay made on me the first time I saw her; it seems to me that there must have been, from the first moments, a kind of complicity between us. Perhaps I even thought: "It is by this woman that I shall be saved!"

We drank a little and we talked. The evening was not very far along when—out of nervousness or exhaustion?—I was seized with a sudden bout of fever which made my teeth chatter. At the

present moment, I have no way of knowing if this attack was real
—provoked by my physical state—or due to my emotion at finding myself with Kay. Most likely I was a victim of that sacred
horror, that sense of paralysis and collapse which still overcomes
me when I am in the presence of love.

I felt so ill that I had to lie down on a couch. Everyone fussed
over me, including Kay, who cared for me with great solicitude.
We left as soon as I had recovered a little, but not before I had
apologized for the grotesque incident and made an appointment
for another evening. My friends took me home in a taxi. Kay
told me afterward that Owl had described me as a great drinker
and had explained my sudden indisposition as an alcoholic
attack.

I was—or thought myself—so exhausted when I again visited
Kay (who lived not far from my own house), that I was obliged
to walk with a cane. Before climbing the stairs to her apartment,
I stopped at a café for a cup of black coffee, hoping to rouse my
strength and stimulate my nerves. When I reached her door I
felt better, Kay appeared pleased to see me in better health, and
our little party was a gay one. There were the kind of records
we liked and—since everywhere we went Owl described us as her
"dancers"—there was no question of doing anything but dancing. At one point I went down to the cellar with Kay for more
bottles of wine; as she walked ahead of me down the stairs, I felt
like kissing the back of her neck, but did not dare. Then, rather
late in the evening, we played a game that involved dressing up:
Kay put on my suit coat, took my cane and my hat, lent me a
dress and various jewels and accessories, and helped me to make
up; Owl and Pinhead exchanged their clothes in the same way.
The two couples then performed various music-hall numbers
and pretended to flirt. I was very proud of being credible instead
of ridiculous as a woman. Every difficulty was solved for me,
since, thanks to my disguise, I had only to let myself go. I therefore took a positive pleasure in this apparent change of sex,
which transformed sexual relations into a game and established

a kind of frivolity. Pretending to woo me, Kay called me by my feminized name—Micheline—a name my mother had planned to give me before I was born, when she had hoped for a daughter. Lying on the couch beside Owl who—sleeping or not?—grinned and kept turning over, we gradually passed from stage kisses to the real thing. Pinhead, who worried more about his health since his fainting fit, had left long since.

At dawn, Owl and I said good night; I took her home and we separated as if nothing had happened.

In the course of the same week, Kay and I met again and danced, this time without disguises. We were, I think, at our dancing club; Kay must have been wearing the hat that I saw so often at the beginning of our affair and that made her look like a swan. The Faun was there, and I was jealous of him, fearing that his professional wrestler's looks would impress this girl who, since the night we had dressed up, I felt was destined to be mine. Fortunately nothing of the kind occurred, and when we left, Kay whispered that I was to come back: her door would be open and all I had to do was turn the handle. Leaving with my friends, I walked a few steps with them in the street, then left them on some pretext or other (which was probably quite transparent) and returned to Kay. She was waiting for me behind her door in a dressing gown, already prepared for the night. We almost immediately fell into each other's arms on the couch, exchanging passionate words and caresses, but when the dreamed-of moment came, my excitement was so great that I proved incapable of the least demonstration of virility.

This occurred on August 7, 1919, and I was eighteen years old. It was only a day or two later, when I had somewhat calmed down, that I actually lost my virginity. Kay, although surprised, had not attributed my initial impotence to timidity but to my fatigue and alcoholism.

FOR eight days, I was in a state of triumph: the world was no longer in its accustomed place, I had found the sorceress by whom everything was transformed, I experienced the sensation of unimagined spiritual intoxication. From the physical point of view, I had never known such transports: my vigor seemed limitless, and I felt I was made to give pleasure continually, and nothing pleased me more than to do so; but I was so little concerned with my own pleasure that it was almost annihilated; sometimes I was even obliged to pretend, and what actually intoxicated me most was the scent of cunning born of this deception, which I deliberately enacted without being at all fooled by myself. Asceticism in fornication, unselfishness in possession, *sacrifice* in pleasure, these were also the ideas whose antinomian appearance exalted me. It required a certain time for me to get used to no longer pretending, to lose myself, to engulf myself in pleasure. Gradually I established both a carnal and an emotional relation. We invented a whole bedroom mythology, and before this love collapsed entirely, it was to last four years. From the first, I had automatically detached myself from my friends Pinhead and Owl.

In the collapse of this liaison intervened several elements I cannot pass over in silence, although it pains me to reveal at least some among them.

FIRST of all, *lassitude,* pure satiety, the desire for change. Love—the only possibility of a coincidence between subject and object, the only means of acceding to the sacred, as represented by the desired object insofar as it is exterior and alien to us—implies its own negation because to possess the sacred is at the same time to profane and finally to destroy it by gradually robbing it of its alien character. A lasting love is a charisma that it takes a long time to exhaust. In mere eroticism, everything is clearer: for desire to remain aroused, it need only change its object. The trouble begins the moment man no longer wants to change objects, or when he tries to domesticate the sacred, keeping it within reach of his hands; when it is no longer enough to worship a sacred object, when he tries—having become a god himself—to be a sacred object for the other person in turn, a sacred object the other person will permanently worship. For, between these two beings, sacred to each other and mutually worshiping each other, there is no longer any possibility of movement save in the direction of profanation, of decadence. The only practical chance of salvation is in a love for a creature so self-centered that, despite an unceasing *rapprochement,* one never reaches the limit of one's possible knowledge of that being; or for someone so endowed with an instinctive coquetry that, however profoundly she loves you, it will seem that she is about to escape at every moment.

NEXT, the *obsession with death,* to which I gradually yielded, contemplating the inevitable decline of this woman who was a few years older than myself. Never, before losing my virginity, had I been preoccupied to such a degree with aging. This obsession came to me apropos of the erotic act which, after a certain time, seemed to me an absurdity, considering the inevitable ugliness of our bodies, though we might contemplate them now without disgust. Hence I came to a kind of mystical state, condemning—in the name of death—physical love in general, without daring to confess to myself that it was one particular love I was wearying of. From this period date my first aspirations to poetry, which seemed to me a refuge, a means of attaining the eternal by escaping old age, and at the same time recovering a safe domain that would be all my own, where my partner could not interfere.

So profound was my longing to escape reality—creating for myself an inviolable asylum where neither death nor my mistress could find me—that I invoked it even in certain plans that affected my daily life. I told Kay, for instance, that I dreamed of living with her in a house with many elements existing only in *trompe-l'oeil: trompe-l'oeil* logs would burn in a *trompe-l'oeil* fireplace; chairs and couches would be painted on the walls, we would sit or lie on the floor, and there would be servants in effigy. The only thing that remained unformulated (and which

I probably desired, moreover, only very obscurely) was that the woman who lived with me in this house would also be only a *trompe-l'oeil* woman.

Kay, irritated by my suggestions (whose real cause she must have suspected), by my withdrawal from her, and jealous of several new friendships which my literary ambitions had led me to form, reproached me for being too intellectual. And naturally, the more I withdrew from her, the more friendships I made, miming love with an all the more sustained and scrupulous deliberation because I was concealing from myself the fact that I actually no longer loved her.

From the beginning of my affair with her—even before this idea had found for its incarnation the image of what Kay would look like in only ten years time—I had suffered, although in a milder fashion, from this obsession with death. "I'd like us to be buried together," I had told Kay one of the first mornings I awakened in her bed, and this sentence must be one of the most genuinely tender I have ever spoken to anyone.

THIS almost religious austerity (a last vestige, perhaps, of the piety of my childhood when, for instance, I would stare for minutes at a time at a holy image on the church wall in vain hopes that it would come alive and flicker its eyelids or give me some other sign which in itself would constitute a miracle) mingled with two other elements—*fear* and *timidity*—which contributed to our disunion by gradually leading me to discover all that was artificial and overrated about my love.

Toward the beginning of our intimacy, one evening when, according to our custom, I was waiting for Kay who had just had dinner with her parents, we were followed by a drunken laborer who made certain remarks that I considered insulting to Kay, and to myself as Kay's lover. I turned around and told him so with the doubtlessly absurd attitude of a young bourgeois who considers himself offended by the crudeness of the manual laborer. Suddenly serious, the man strode toward me, swinging his enormous fists, and instinctively I retreated. Supposing he was going to strike me, Kay stood between us, threatening the man with her umbrella. Matters went no further, but I was terribly humiliated.

Another time, leaving Kay and walking home around two in the morning, I was assaulted. Walking on the left-hand sidewalk, I paid no attention to two individuals who had walked past me in the other direction on the opposite side of the street; suddenly two other men coming toward me on my side of the street were standing right in front of me. But the first two men, having crossed the street, now cut off my retreat and each grabbed one of my arms while one of the newcomers pressed a revolver against my chest and the other searched me. "Don't say a word! If you keep quiet we won't hurt you!" I obeyed. It was summer and I had no undershirt on: I distinctly felt the cold metal of the gun barrel against my skin. The four men relieved me of my money, but kindly left me my papers. "Now get out of here!" Actually, it was they who ran off as fast as they could. The incident had occurred so quickly that I was not frightened until afterward. I went on my way and, only a short distance from my home, met some people I knew to whom I told the story, having at the time no intention of doing anything about it. They insisted I inform the police, and the next day I went to the local station; an officer with a smooth-shaven face and a huge watch chain declared he would investigate the case, at the same time dismissing my story: "Petty thieves. . . . Were you afraid of their revolver? It probably wasn't even loaded!" Once again, I felt humiliated.

Since I spent all my evenings with Kay and returned late at night, the possibility of a nocturnal assault had never even occurred to me; moreover, I had always been something of a noctambulist myself. But from this moment, the apprehension of my return somewhat spoiled my pleasure at being with Kay. This changed nothing in our relationship, but I got in the habit of returning by taxi, although each time I did so I was furious with myself for not walking home, for not being freed from terror (in this case, quite chimerical) by my love for Kay. One evening when she had come to our house, in the absence of my father and mother, I even hoped she would leave early, knowing I would have to accompany her and, being short of cash, return on foot. It was that night, upon my return, that I locked myself in the bathroom, took the nail-scissors and lacerated my flesh to punish myself.

Further I suffered greatly from my timidity. Many members of my family (or friends of my family) had seen me with Kay and had gossiped about us. This made it unpleasant for me to accompany her to certain places where I knew we would be noticed. Moreover, her divorce having been decided against her (partly because she had notoriously compromised herself with me), her means of support were greatly reduced; she had to leave her apartment and we could see each other only at hotels. The simple fact of having to ask for a room became a phobia for me; our meetings were poisoned by it. And I was increasingly obsessed by the idea that since my love could not overcome such trifles, I was incapable of loving and too cowardly to deserve being loved.

WHILE I was doing my military service—quite docilely, volunteering for nothing but as much freedom as possible, and much more often taken for an idiot than an intellectual—I agreed to marry Kay. No one in my family would oppose the match. But no sooner had I made this decision than I felt I was in an abyss: I would have to choose a job, support this woman older than myself who would be tied to me forever. No longer emotionally free, and obliged to lead an arduous and mediocre existence, I would also have to renounce that poetic activity to which—precisely because it constituted a realm where I could escape Kay's hold over me—I so longed to abandon myself. In other words, I would escape my military service only to be burdened at once with still heavier chains.

My new curiosity about art, in what seemed to me its "modern" expression, having led me to the Ballet Russe, I had seen a performance of *Petrouchka*, and I compared myself to the puppet imprisoned in his star-painted box which he beats with both fists, before collapsing, conquered by this metaphysical barrier.

I basely swallowed my scruples about the detrimental role I had played in Kay's divorce, telling myself that I had had nothing to do with it, that it was she—after all—who had "seduced" me. But I was ashamed of these thoughts, clinging to my love and supposing that if I were really in love no such considerations should make me hesitate.

MY FATHER had died over a year before, on a snowy day, following an operation. Always fond of music, he had insisted, knowing he was close to the end, on my brother's playing a tune he loved on his violin. Then, a day or two later, saying that he saw snow around him, and that he "wanted heaps of it," he died, his eyes fixed on my mother's. This profound, timeless love, which had persisted to the end between them, made me all the more aware of my own infamy. It was after this incident that I had resolved to get married, despite my real inclinations.

The breakup occurred apropos of the vacation I wanted to spend with some of the new friends of whom Kay, quite rightly, was jealous. During a walk in the Bois, it was I who took the initiative, declaring in utter dismay to Kay that I no longer loved her.

HOLOFERNES' FEAST

A FEW months later, I ended my military service with almost as much sadness as joy, for I felt that now I had reached manhood and that the time was past when I could *do nothing* with impunity. Determined to devote all my energy to literature, I followed my vocation and—renouncing the vague scientific studies which I had hitherto pursued—left the chemistry laboratory without even saying good-by to my instructors.

Poetry had replaced the mysticism in which I had floundered

after my breakup with Kay. I believed in nothing—in any case not in God or another life—but I blithely talked about the Absolute, the Eternal, and I believed that man had the power to transmute everything by the lyrical use of words. I accorded a preponderant importance to the *imaginary* as a substitute for the real, a world in which we have the capacity to create. The poet seemed to me a predestined man, a kind of demiurge whose obligation was to effect the mental transformation of the universe, which was true only to the degree one chose to attribute truth to it. I believed that by means of words it was possible to detect ideas, so that from one unforeseen verbal shock to the next, one could encircle the Absolute more and more closely and finally, by releasing new ideas in all directions, possess it. The poet also seemed to me—necessarily—a condemned man, damned and doomed for all eternity to a miserable solitude and having as his only spiritual recourse this constant hunger, product of complete and irremediable dissatisfaction.

I was chaste, for I now believed that any authentic love was out of the question. Perhaps, more than anything else, I found such an attitude a convenient means of suppressing my obsessions. This is what I think now that I have considered myself a little more closely, struggled to reject my pretensions, and tried to reduce everything to its true proportions.

I tended to a kind of asceticism, setting poetic fervor above all else and showing some indulgence only for alcohol, which I would question like an oracle and which I prized as an instrument of madness, a virulent poison which detaches us from reality, illusorily endowing us with a kind of heroic strength and a demigod's intangibility.

I believed I was a desperate man. Resentful of the fact that I had been brought into the world, I rebelled against the laws of the material universe, railed against weight and substance, the resistance of matter, the change of the seasons. It was only long afterward that, quite intellectually and by indirect means, I shifted from this essential rebellion—or rather from this rejection—to the notion of political revolution. I did not quite admit to myself then that what aroused my fury against life was not the condition which the natural and social laws had created, but simply death; I vaguely hoped that the poetic miracle would intervene to change everything, and that I would enter into "eternity" alive, having conquered my destiny as a man with the help of words. I also—and contradictorily—retained a vague image of happiness, of a purely human Paradise, like the one from my earliest childhood to which an everlasting mutual love would give us the key. I preserved in the deepest part of my being this calm, gentle Utopia like an illustration from a children's book, and if I regarded myself as a doomed man, it was actually because I was sure this Eden would be pitilessly denied me rather than because of any contempt I might have entertained toward such happiness.

I had already been concerned with my appearance for some time, attaching an almost maniacal importance to the arrangement of my clothes. As much as possible, I affected the English manner, preferring this sober and correct style—actually a little stiff and even funereal—which corresponds so well, I believe, to my temperament.

Because my skin was frequently irritated by the razor, I had got into the habit of powdering my face (and this since I was fifteen), as if I were trying to conceal it under a mask and afford my person an impassivity like that of plaster. This corresponded to a symbolic attempt at mineralization, a defense-reaction against my inner weakness and the collapse by which I felt myself threatened; I longed for some kind of armor, seeking to achieve in my eternal *persona* the same idea of stiffness and rigidity which I pursued poetically.

Other details of adornment permitted me to satisfy that predilection for "eccentricity" which had not left me, as well as to express that tendency to an icy hardness by which my literary attempts were still marked, at least in some respects. Thus, for a while, I wore a tight wire instead of a watchband; my lapel was

decorated with a piece of barbed wire instead of the usual ribbon; at the same time—passionately eager to identify myself
with the world by dissolving my limits or by incorporating it—
I planned to cover my whole body with astral tattoos that would
have illustrated—by their very presence on my skin—this attempted fusion of microcosm with macrocosm. Later, I had my
head shaved and asked a painter friend of mine to take a razor
and draw a part that would start at the back of my neck and
run down to the middle of my forehead—an image of the geometrical *figura* I wanted to be, a kind of divine Adam or constellation.

Whatever the distinctly speculative role I then assigned to
poetry, I took a certain sensual pleasure in the manipulation of
language—enjoying the weight and savor of words, dissolving
them in my mouth like fruits—and this pleasure prevailed, in
the hierarchy of my preoccupations, over any strictly erotic delights. From the emotional point of view, friendship was enough
for me—an ideal secret society, an intimate alliance of a few individuals, in perfect communion of views, of life, and of labor,
in the sordid studio where we met, its moldy walls covered with
cockroaches which served the function of extending our conversations by preventing us from sleeping. Among these friends,
one of whom was more or less my mentor and had a decisive influence on my spiritual formation, I had found again—more
validly established, and more intense—the extraordinary climate
of moral community which I had already experienced with my
companions Pinhead and Owl. It was also my first precise contact with one thing that was entirely new for me: poverty.

Just as my affair with Kay had marked the end of a first experience in friendship, my marriage—without separating me from
my new circle—has nonetheless constituted a sufficiently profound modification of this climate for me to suffer from it even
today and, in my hours of depression, to yearn for it as for a
Paradise Lost.

Of this period, which began with my first literary productions,

I shall give only a brief account, for I am still too deeply involved in it to be able to treat it with much discernment and *sang-froid*.

I HAVE never written with facility, and indeed for a long time it never occurred to me that I might some day be what is called a writer. The first modern poet whose acquaintance I had made (a man whom I admired at least as much as Apollinaire) had often discouraged me, urging me to continue my studies and not aspire to be anything more than an "honest man" or, at the most, a "distinguished amateur." I gibed at this counsel, which I regarded as without appeal; I had expected from this man not moral advice, but a formula and a key, and would have gone to the point of sharing his vices if that had been the means of acquiring his genius. Convinced, moreover, that a great artist is necessarily doomed to poverty, I blushed at my own comfort, holding it responsible for everything and reproaching myself for not having the energy to give it all up.

I was not to succeed in producing anything readable until I met the painter André Masson and he expressed his confidence in me, as did the small group of intimate friends who met in his studio. Still, I have never been able to work except discontinuously, in flashes, and struggling at every step of the way against the worst difficulties.

Poetic inspiration seemed to me an altogether rare piece of luck, a momentary gift from heaven which it was the poet's responsibility to be in a state to receive by means of an absolute purity, and by paying with his misery for the fortuitous benefit of this manna. I regarded the lyric state as a kind of trance; I would remain overwhelmed, mute, scarcely answering questions, as if I were only concerned with whatever was happening inside me that took the form of a harsh, grating, rusty poetry torturing my vitals like a foreign body, or huddled in some foresaken corner of my head like that material soul in whose existence I had believed as a child. Receptivity necessitated all kinds of precautions in order to be safeguarded, for the least thing could destroy it forever; a single compromise was enough, a lack of detachment, any concession at all in the direction of happiness, to which one might yield as to a sin. Convinced that the exercise of poetry required an enormous proportion of freedom and courage and implied, above all, a perfect disinterestedness in temporal relationships, I meditated on Gobineau's fable (one of the *Nouvelles Asiatiques*) of the initiate to whom an illustrious thaumaturge is about to reveal the ultimate magical secret, but who loses everything on the threshold of discovery because he turns back when his wife (who saw herself being abandoned) follows and calls to him.

Thus, when love appeared in my thoughts, it was in the form of a temptation, and I could not envisage it save as a kind of failure. Nonetheless it was under these conditions—as if I had committed a kind of treason or at least made a bitter renunciation—that I got married.

A young girl in the circle I now belonged to, thanks to the new orientation I had given my life—a girl very strictly brought up—suddenly appeared to me the incarnation or the reflection of that picture-book image that I secretly nourished within myself, an image that had retreated into the depths of childhood romance, which endowed it with an overwhelming glamour by all its distant and legendary character.

Because I was embarrassed by her evidently bourgeois education, paralyzed by a sudden return of all my phobias, and convinced, moreover, that if I married the possibility of friendship would vanish, I behaved toward her in the most unbelievably conventional manner. First I officially asked for her hand, then I did not dare to court her save by sending her bouquets and poems and turned cold and silent as soon as I was alone with her. She refused me.

I cast this unfortunate adventure outside the circle of my preoccupations. I congratulated and almost glorified myself on my failure, convinced that marriage and poetry were mutually exclusive.

I was no longer concerned with anything except writing, and I was soon participating deeply in the modern literary movement.

This was the period when I spent most of my nights in Montmartre, hanging around night clubs like Zelli's and preferring the Negro bars to all the rest. I had new friends with whom I drank and philosophized, for drink, smoke, music, and crowds constituted the mental stimulants we considered most favorable to inspiration. Quite often I got drunk, more convinced than ever of alcohol's value and appreciating, moreover, the bittersweet flavor of cocktails, the snowy taste of champagne, and the sharp tang of whiskey. With regard to women, I remained chaste, or almost so. As in the days when I went from one party to the next with Pinhead and Owl, I suffered from a certain emptiness, but this boredom had soon become the source of inexpressible emotions whenever I heard a jazz tune that was suitably melancholy or blues sung by a colored woman whose throat seemed to have been pecked by a bird.

Many of our afternoons were spent in movie theaters. We favored the facile sentimentality of American comedies, or else those violent films in which respectable men are destroyed and derelicts rehabilitated by falling into a woman's arms—bold heroes for whom ruin and redemption were one, since in one case as in the other the climax consisted of the same elementary leap which takes a man *outside himself.*

Knowing my chastity was more the effect of an incurable deficiency than of will, and perhaps the logical consequence of a simple incapacity to love, I was crushed with shame by the thought of adventures spoiled because of my timidity, or by the realization that I had even thought of marrying so bourgeois a girl in so bourgeois a fashion. I recovered a certain amount of pride only in the conviction that despite all my weaknesses, I was living *as a poet:* wandering about the streets at night, dreaming and often delirious, doomed to failure since there could be no common denominator between the world and himself.

There was another, more material cause for this sense of impotence, one which made almost any sexual relation with women impossible for me, and this was a benign infirmity—which no treatment till now has succeeded in healing—a slight strain in one testicle. This had happened following a great period of exhaustion, after several virtually sleepless nights of speculation over some vague plan—between passion, mysticism, and lyricism—with the homosexual friend of whom I have spoken apropos of the various incarnations of Judith.

Of course, I would be overestimating the impression which certain dreams of classical mythology made upon me in my early youth if I said that they constituted for my imagination—as soon as I was aware of them—an aliment comparable to that which I later derived from operas or from films, or to that which films afford me today. All the same, there are two which profoundly impressed me and which I have returned to subsequently: the fall of Icarus, and Phaëthon struck by Zeus's thunderbolt because, as he drove Apollo's chariot he came too close to the earth, disobeying the instructions he had received from his father. In the picture book where I first read the legend of Phaëthon, Phoebus was represented in a Louis XIV costume and called, I believe, "Le Roi Soleil"; perhaps this additional detail—reminding me of the Palace of Versailles and situating Phaëthon and his father in the framework of French history—has helped imprint on my memory a narrative which I already had good reasons to recall. For indeed I was many times preoccupied by this myth, and it has often served as the substance of my dreams.

At the period when I made the acquaintance of this friend who was certainly a worthier companion than I to inflict a kind of Luciferian transfiguration upon existence, I imagined that I had, still more than a vocation, a *destiny,* for the state of exaltation in which I found myself seemed to me an irrefutable proof that my life had something mythical about it. Conscious as I was of the mediocrity of my literary means, I regarded myself as a kind of prophet, and I derived a great deal of pride from a messianism which seemed to me inherent in the fate of any poet. It was something like the wings of Icarus or the horses of Phaëthon.

Speaking sometimes in complete darkness in order to convince ourselves we were outside of space, free of all material relations (as if we were moving in the absolute, mirrored in one another and exchanging crucifixions in our double solitude), my friend and I had carried our conversations to a point that might pass for a violation of the taboo, a sacrilege. So it seemed to me only natural that I should incur punishment. "I am punished even in my flesh," I wrote, as soon as the physical suffering in question was manifested.

By reason of its mythical value and because it seemed to me impossible that a poet should be anything but *doomed* (Icarus, Prometheus, or Phaëthon), the belief that I was the fire-stealer, doomed to an eternal vulture, permitted me of course to live, combined with a passion for travel—for I was convinced that I would one day "set out." I was humiliated, however, by my genital defect, as I had been by my head injury as a child, when I had supposed myself disfigured and wondered: "How can I make love?" This resulted in a constant *malaise* which immersed me deeper and deeper in my conviction of weakness and cowardice.

One day—around the beginning of July, 1925—I managed to accomplish what my circle generally considered an act of bravura: at the end of a literary banquet which ended in a fight, I was roughed up by the police and almost got lynched, having made seditious speeches and defied police and crowd alike. Actually, I had previously doped myself with the help of two or three *apéritifs*, so great had been my fear that I would not seem courageous. For virtually a week I had to stay in my room, for I was still in shock from the beating I had suffered; for a while I figured as a sort of minor hero among my friends, which satisfied both my desire for expiation and my need to feel admired.

This did not keep my depression from increasing. Decompos-
ing the words of the vocabulary and reconstructing them in
poetic puns which seemed to me to explain their deepest mean-
ings, dreaming and writing down my dreams, regarding some as
revelations whose metaphysical bearing I had to discover, comparing them in order to decipher their meaning and deriving
from them all sorts of narratives, I woke up screaming almost
every night. Sometimes I dreamed that, since speech and breath
are inseparably linked, my experiments with language had
caused me to lose my power of speech and that to keep from
smothering—i.e., to *cure* myself—I had been forced to drink a
violent poison which would make me *die* in terrible agony.
Sometimes I imagined the earth isolated in space, not as the dead
image of a globe, but in a living manner; and I perceived its
crust, its roughness. Sometimes there was a helmeted Roman
profile with the features of a medal (a true head of Holofernes,
even to a beard), which appeared to me as the very image of my
sleep as well as the symbol of death by decapitation.

A relationship with a strange person who had recently come
into our circle—a defrocked seminarist who was a mythomaniac
combined with an adventurer—managed to unbalance me completely. Having long hoped to be dissolved in a kind of deliberate madness (like what I assumed Gérard de Nerval's to have
been) I was suddenly seized with a terrible fear of going truly
mad. It would be a punishment for these inhuman longings for
unreason and for my attempts—raising the veil of Isis—to pene-
trate the mysteries by force.

One day I was walking with the ex-seminarist on the boulevards when he indicated someone who was walking behind us,
declaring that this person had pointed at him and called him a
"wizard"; the following night I was seized with a panic agony so
severe that I had to ask my mother to let me sleep in her room.

The next day, I was to leave for the south, accompanied by
the young girl I had so stupidly courted a year and a half before;
having remained on excellent terms with her family, I was in-

vited to join them in their car for the trip. This automobile excursion was a delicious diversion for me: I relaxed, the two of us talked a great deal, and no sooner had we reached the Riviera than we announced our engagement.

Everything went so simply that once again I did not have the sense of having *conquered,* but rather that of having been the plaything of events. Around my eyes, I kept the traces of the blows I had received: the sign of the coward's redemption, which gives him the right to be loved, but also the last vestige of that *mauvais garçon* who—so prosaically—was on the road to good behavior. What brought this feeling of stupidity to its peak was the fact that my fiancée and I did not make love before our legal marriage, whatever the freedom of our beach life and that of the return trip, which I foolishly did not even try to take advantage of.

Knowing what part my sudden fear of solitude had played in this, I secretly blamed myself with subtle vehemence for having abandoned my Promethean pedestal and returned to mediocrity by the most ordinary bourgeois marriage. I also feared, on account of that physical affliction I have mentioned, that I would display only a pathetic virility, and it seemed to me that at scarcely twenty-four I was already touched by that premonitory sign of old age: no longer able to make love without being obsessed by the idea that I might not be able to make love adequately. Consequently it seemed that all my behavior was nothing but a base swindle in regard to this woman who was about to share my days and nights, and this merely increased my remorse, so liable to turn, as is customary, into pure hostility.

On February 2, 1926, our civil marriage was performed, we invited no one, and this completed the rupture between certain members of my family and myself, by which I was not at all affected. Yet this idea of failure inherent, as I saw it, in marriage was to haunt me constantly and even now I often wonder if the woman one lives with, the image of what one has desired, is not —however worthy of love she may be—one's daily reproach for not having aimed *too* high, for having been able to be content.

Therefore, since this event, I have unceasingly felt myself to be Hercules at Omphale's spinning wheel, Samson shorn by Delilah, in other words, still less than Holofernes' head when it ignominiously lies in blood and sour wine, beside the spattered dress of a romantic Judith.

VIII

The Raft of the Medusa

MEDUSA (*The Raft of the*), masterpiece by Géricault
(Salon of 1819), at the Musée du Louvre. —The artist has
chosen the moment which precedes the rescue. On the
clumsy raft, at the waves' mercy, the last survivors are
clustered at the foot of the improvised mast; Corréard
(who later published a narrative of the shipwreck), his
arm outstretched, is showing a brig on the horizon to
the surgeon Savigny, who is standing with his back to
the mast, and to the sailors; a Negro hoisted onto a cask
waves a shred of cloth. An old man holds the body of his
son on his knees.

This work, remarkable for its skillful composition, the
realism of its expression, the scale of its drawing, and
finally the brilliance of its coloring, was not understood
when it was first shown. The painter was unable to sell
his canvas, which he decided to take with him to
England.

This disaster inspired Charles Desnoiers and Dennery
to write a drama in five acts and six scenes (Ambigu-
Comique, 1839), whose settings by Philastre and Cam-
bon assured its great success.

(*Nouveau Larousse Illustré*)

IN NOVEMBER 1929, after various disappointments and disasters dating back to the spring before (consistently abortive attempts at love; scandalous drunkenness; almost
bloody bites inflicted on my hands by a woman with whom I
had once been in love; all-night debauchery after which, having
been unable to achieve my purpose with a little American Negro
dancer, I appeared at a friend's house around five in the morning
and asked to borrow his razor with the—more or less sham—intention of castrating myself, a request my friend evaded by informing me that all he had was an electric razor), I realized that
disease played a part in every one of these manifestations, and
I decided to undertake psychoanalytic treatment.

I did not consider myself as sexually perverted; but I had reached the point of no longer being able to function at all. Among other things I was suffering a thousand agonies to complete on schedule the articles I was writing for a periodical, and I realized, on a more serious plane, that I resembled a clown more than a tragic actor. Above all, I wanted to free myself of that hideous sense of impotence—as much genital as intellectual —from which I still suffer today.

The stories of even the least glittering debauches which stud a part of this narrative never represent anything *vile* for me, in the strict sense of the word; they simply correspond to failures, i.e., to attempts at freedom which are ultimately pathetic and clumsy, from which I derive no pleasure—or only a limited pleasure—instead of the extreme delight I had hoped would be as pure and direct as the sudden light that dawns in the poet's mind, or the lightning-like sword stroke by which the matador dispatches his adversary.

In a general way of speaking, sadism, masochism, etc., do not constitute "vices" for me, but only means of attaining a more intense reality. In love, everything always seems too gratuitous, too anodyne, too lacking in gravity; the punishment of social disgrace, of blood or death must intervene to make the game worth the candle. Thus practices which involve physical suffering, although affording love this gravity to a certain degree, can only disgust me once I know that they will remain factitious and that I will not dare carry them, like Lucrece, to the point of suicide, or like Judith, to that of slaughter.

By psychoanalysis, I hoped to free myself from this chimerical fear of punishment, a chimera reinforced by the absurd power of Christian morality—which one must never flatter oneself that one has altogether escaped—and the constraint of illogical and inhuman conventions characteristic of a civilization that kills the criminals it produces and solves by destruction or warfare such problems as overproduction and unemployment.

I have undergone this treatment for about a year with various results. It was, at least during the first period, salt on my wounds. One drunken night, I slept with a half-mad elderly alcoholic Englishwoman; even as I was pumping her, I had a furious desire to break or steal her pearl necklace, merely in order to play the brute; between embraces, we each drank a huge glass of whiskey out of her toothbrush glass. I certainly never loved her, but I was, for a long time afterward, fascinated by her. On another occasion, in a brothel, convinced that the only authentic reaction I could expect from a prostitute was an expression of the hatred she could not fail to feel toward me, I made her and the madam slap me until my face was black and blue; enjoying themselves, the two women, when they saw me grinning, struck me all the harder, saying: "You ready for some more, you old bugger?"

One day, visiting a couple I admire (the wife for her extraordinary sweetness, the husband because he seemed to me the prototype of the traveler), I met a short blonde woman from the country, wearing mourning for a child she had just lost; I decided then and there to make her. I actually had no real desire to do so, but she fascinated me simply because she was in mourning, because she had talked about the boredom of provincial life, and about those madwomen that are called *aboyeuses* in Brittany because they howl like dogs, about adultery in which it is bad to indulge because it disturbs the "general order," about her fear of spiders, which counterbalanced her interest in tropical countries, about the seaport she lived in, where the shipowners are so hard on the "poor sailors." I spent only a few hours with her, kissed her on the mouth in a taxi, and left her in hysterics in front of a drygoods store where she was planning to shop; I never saw her again. She never answered the letter in which I proposed a meeting, and several days later, I wandered drunkenly through the streets, entering various apartment houses, walking up as far as the fifth floor, and asking neighborhood bartenders if they had seen this woman whose name I no longer remember today.

Coming out of this limbo, advised by my doctor and con-

vinced myself that I needed a more strenuous life for a while, I
seized the opportunity of making a long trip and went to Africa
for almost two years, as a member of an ethnographical expedi-
tion. After months of chastity and emotional weaning, I fell in
love while in Gondar with an Ethiopian woman who corresponded physically and morally to my double image of Lucrece
and Judith. Her face beautiful but her breasts ravaged, she was
wrapped in a filthy gray toga, smelled of sour milk, and owned a
young Negro slave girl; she looked like a wax statue, and the
bluish tattoos around her neck set off her head like a transparent
collar or the carcan of an old rack. Perhaps she was only a new
image—in flesh and blood this time—of that Marguerite with the
severed head whose ghost I never managed to glimpse at the
opera, as a child. She was a syphilitic and had several times produced stillborn children. Her first husband had gone mad; the
most recent, on two occasions, had tried to kill her. Her clitoris
extirpated, like all the women of her race, she must have been
frigid, at least from a European point of view. The daughter
of a kind of witch possessed by many spirits, she would, according to rumor, inherit these spirits, some of which had already
afflicted her with disease, thereby marking her out as their ineluctable prey. When she killed a white ram and dedicated it to
one of these genies, I saw her gasping in a trance—in a state of
complete possession—and drinking, out of a porcelain cup, the
victim's blood still hot from the slit throat. I never made love
to her, but when the sacrifice took place it seemed to me that
a relation more intimate than any carnal link was established
between her and myself. After I left Gondar, I had various
chance encounters with Somali girls in the native quarter of
Djibout; yet these *amours*, however absurd and unfortunate,
have left me with an impression of Paradise.

In 1933 I returned, having killed at least one myth: that of
travel as a means of escape. I have subsequently gone back to
therapy twice, once for only a brief period of time. The chief
thing I have learned from it is that, even in what first appear

to be the most heterogeneous manifestations, one always finds that one is oneself, that there is a unity in life, and that everything leads back, whatever one does, to a specific constellation of things which one tends to reproduce, under various forms, an unlimited number of times. I am in better health, apparently, and am no longer as continuously haunted by the "tragic themes" and by the idea that I can do nothing that will not humiliate me. I measure my preferences by their true value, I no longer abandon myself to those ridiculous follies, yet everything happens exactly as if the fallacious constructions on which I based my life had been undermined at their source without anything having been given me to replace them. As a result, I act, certainly, with more sagacity, but the void in which I move is all the more apparent. With a bitterness I did not used to suspect, I have come to realize that only a certain fervor could save me, but that this world has nothing in it *for which I am capable of dying.*

Always beneath or above concrete events, I remain a prisoner of this alternative: the world as a real object which dominates and devours me (like Judith) in suffering and in fear, or else the world as a pure fantasy which dissolves in my hands, which I destroy (like Lucrece thrusting home the dagger) without ever succeeding in possessing it. Perhaps, above all, the question for me is to escape this dilemma by finding a way in which the world and myself—object and subject—confront each other on an equal footing, as the matador stands before the bull.

I have scrutinized the data my analysis afforded me and compared, specifically, the incident of the dispute with my father apropos of Apollinaire's lines to a dream I had years later: An ideal father, to whom (in the dream) I am linked by an ambiguous relationship, kills me because I have performed an act equivalent to my emancipation—that is, symbolically, to his murder, in order to supplant him and acquire his virility, like Oedipus killing Laius before marrying Jocasta. By this comparison (of dream and memory) I manage to understand somewhat better what the figure of Judith means for me, the image of that punishment simultaneously feared and desired: castration.

And if I think at the same time of the depressing influence my Catholic education has had on my whole development—chiefly the notion of *forbidden fruit* and, still more, that of *original sin* (which I know still obsesses me, however certain I am of having broken intellectually with this kind of prejudice)—I now understand quite clearly my sense of guilt—no longer *hidden,* like the kind derived from childhood images of the consequences of masturbation or of incest desires, but somehow *effective*. At the same time "confession" exercises an imperious attraction on my mind—by its humiliating aspect, combined with all that is scandalous and exhibitionistic about it—and I still behave like a kind of "damned soul" eternally pursued by his punishment, suffering from it but asking nothing better than to bring this curse to its excruciating climax. This is an attitude from which I have long derived a delight as intense as it is severe. Eroticism is necessarily placed, for me, under the sign of torment, of ignominy and, still more, of terror. Obviously these are my most violent excitation factors since they alone, by reason of their painful content, permit me to regard my tithe as paid and to enjoy myself freely, since by discharging my debt I have suppressed the stupid obsession of original sin.

Gradually a kind of dead calm has replaced these tempests; but in recent months, I note that I may be committing myself to a new inferno, less flamboyant, more trivial, but just as unendurable. Here, whatever the case, is the tenor of this dream of "emancipation":

MAY 8, 1925—I am in the African division with my friend the painter André Masson (who was, in actuality, a kind of spiritual father to me). Older than I, Masson has *every* privilege over my person. Having somehow outlawed myself by adopting a nihilistic ideology that denies all values and all morality—an ideology still more negative than that of my friends—I am no longer entitled to any consideration, and can be nothing but an *object of amusement* (a "scapegoat") to my friends. While we are working as road menders, André Masson amuses himself by stoning me, the pebbles he throws getting larger and larger. I try to avoid these projectiles; I throw them back; it becomes a David and Goliath battle, but less fortunate than David, I am wounded by an enormous stone that grazes my temple, and I fall stunned. My mentor André Masson has just murdered me.

That night, I awakened with a shriek. Did this shriek, I still wonder today, express the most terrible agony or a shattering pleasure?

ABOUT a year and a half ago, being on terms of erotic intimacy with a woman of foreign origin who—I later realized—was making fun of me, I had a series of dreams in which a certain number of my obsessions seemed to be condensed. I had considered her first of all as nothing but a flirtatious and mannered girl, until the day I suddenly realized that she had a child of her own, which affected me as a kind of monstrosity, considering the fragility of her physical structure. For reasons I need not go into here, my wife was bedridden at the time, but instead of arousing my sympathies her affliction merely constrained me all the more. From the group of dreams which were at least the indirect transposition of these events, I extract the following two most recent apparitions of Judith and Lucrece.

THE TURBAN-WOMAN

IN AN apparently colonial country, I am participating in a conspiracy and engaged in smuggling with a friend (a boy I encountered, in real life, at the meetings of a political circle to which I belonged). There are two routes: one, in two stages, that is longer; the other, in a single stage, that is shorter but more exhausting. We are walking along a narrow, dusty path with steep banks on either side; as we walk we notice objects such as

masks and primitive sculptures lying about on the ground, but
we do not bother to pick them up. When we reach our destination, we are in a sordid colonial city: the air is sultry, there is a
red sun and fog. Men in khaki shorts are walking through the
streets, ill-shaven and dirty; one huge fat man, with his wife and
children, seems particularly disgusting. Then, after a scene in
a café which is the rendezvous of the conspirators and the smugglers, I am sitting at my American desk (a piece of furniture
which I actually possess and on which I am writing at this moment). On a large sheet of paper I have patiently drawn signs
that look like commas or Arabic letters; it is the laborious work
of several months or years. I realize that this paper is a piece of
cloth and that a mouth which happens to be drawn on it near the
top (no doubt by the accidental configuration of a group of signs)
makes of it a woman's face. I then roll the piece of cloth around
my head like a turban and remain frozen in this position, my
chest bare, sitting in front of my desk in ecstasy, like a kind of
fakir (or—as it now occurs to me—a rajah like the one who
stabbed himself, after first having his wives killed). Ghostly in a
long white nightgown, my wife is standing beside me. Seeing me
put on the turban, she murmurs with unspeakable sadness (as if
she had finally discovered the meaning of what I had been doing
for so long, the result of the signs I was accumulating one by
one): "Oh! So that was it. . . ." Still in ecstasy, I decide there is
now nothing left to do but die. I stretch out my hand toward
the right-hand drawer of my desk, a drawer where—in the dream
as in reality—my revolver is kept. But the movement that I make
to take hold of the revolver brings the ecstasy to an end and
wakes me up.

I realized the next day that the turban-woman was in fact my
mistress, whom I had helped to retie her turban the day before.
As for the piece of cloth covered with signs and animated by a
mouth, I discovered somewhat later what had suggested it: the
image of the Venetian blinds in my bedroom (in the apartment
my wife and I shared at the time with my mother), a multiple

colonnade of slats with a tear in one of them toward the top that
looked like a mouth which gaped at me each morning and sometimes seemed to be kissing.

THE BLEEDING NAVEL

I LEAVE a public place where there has been a demonstration
such as an official marriage or ceremony, my right arm around
the same mistress. My elder brother (the one I don't like) is walking beside us and telling me things which do not interest me at
all; he speaks only to me, behaving—intentionally or not—as if
my mistress were not there. I myself pay attention only to her;
the two of us are isolated: for us, it is as if the outer world did
not exist; for the outer world, it is as if we ourselves did not exist,
and perhaps this is why my brother does not see her. My mistress talks to me about our isolation, our singularity in relation
to other couples.

We now find ourselves at the stairway to a Métro station,
facing each other, near the curved cast-iron balustrade; we are
quarreling. Distressed at having quarreled, we are reconciled,
but words are not enough to efface this distress; therefore, for
the first time, very tenderly, we kiss each other. One of us, or
both, says prophetically: "One day we'll fight; we'll make
up. . . ." The kiss is very sweet.

The scene changes: we are now alone in the bedroom of a
small apartment. The decoration of this room is gloomy, with a
faded, ordinary wallpaper; it looks like a poor scholar's study.
My mistress is lying on a couch naked, having kept on only the
boots she wears on rainy days. I am caressing her breasts. I see
her belly which looks strained, swollen; I notice a tiny puddle
of blood in her navel; I feel a lacerating pity, an immense tenderness, as if her secret wound had been revealed. With a piece of
cotton I tenderly wipe away the blood. Then—apparently—I
bury my head between her thighs.

The dream continues in the most banal reality. The last image

is a kind of tract distributed to his workmen by a Socialist en-
trepreneur. At the bottom of the paper is drawn a pair of high-
button shoes in a style which suggests certain old cobbler signs.

In a dream following this one the same night, I take my mistress home. With her is her sister—a rather vulgar girl whom
I seem to have courted in the past—and perhaps one of my
friends. We're walking in twos, some distance apart. Just before
we reach our destination in a new street with comfortable houses
(the street lamps are electric), my mistress says something like
this: "I am quite fond of you (*meaning that she is fond of me but
only somewhat*) but, frankly, I don't like the way you dress." I
am upset; I think of the hat I'm wearing (whereas so many men
go out bareheaded), of the bowler I used to have, of my belted
raincoat, my gloves, my mannered look, of all that it represents,
of my constraint, etc. . . . I know that I cannot change and
that even if I tried to change, I would only forfeit her esteem.

I explain to my mistress how necessary it is to construct a wall
around oneself by means of clothing.

NOTES

Page 3, line 1: *I have just reached the age of thirty-four* . . .

I will be thirty-five when these pages are published for the first time. Such a gap would justify a new book. I offer only these hurried notes, reduced to the indispensable.

Page 22, line 29: . . . *what torture endure* . . .

This question of resistance to physical pain—a question which has always obsessed me, but only theoretically—acquired a grim reality during the period of police terror imposed by the German occupation. There remains like a shadow on my conscience the certainty that, if I had ever been arrested and tortured, I should never have had the strength, in the hands of my torturers, to keep from "talking."

Page 23, line 2: . . . *in whose third act* . . .

Actually the fourth act, not the third.

Page 35, line 12: . . . *Molière, all of whose works I detest* . . .

Having attended a performance of *L'Avare* in January, 1941 (a moment, it is true, when everyone deliberately turned back to the French classics, as during all the years of the Occupation), I took great pleasure in this performance and revised my opinion of Molière, which had already been modified when I saw *Tartuffe*. What strikes me about a play by Molière in performance is—and this is rather rare in the theater—the language that one *hears:* the vivid, concrete vocabulary, each word of which crosses the footlights, while the action, exploding in all directions, flares up on the boards.

Page 40, line 9: . . . *the public's attitude at this moment is a religious attitude* . . .

The exit of the dead bull's carcass, drawn by mules or horses to the cracking of whips wielded by the arena attendants, today seems to me to suggest a carnival rather than a religious festival. It is true that the circus, which has more or less retained its parodic meaning, is a celebration of religious origin.

Page 41, line 24: . . . *a good* descabello . . .

I did not know at the time that the *descabello* is only a *coup de grâce;* today, I would no longer speak of a "good" *descabello.* As for the young matador from Seville discussed a few lines below, I believe that if it were possible for me to see him again today, I would be furious with myself for having praised his performance.

Page 63, line 29: . . . *the bloody wrist* . . .

When I saw this wound, it suggested a fresh fig split open. Or, at least, it is of this wound that I now think when I see a split fig.

Page 116, line 16: . . . *her licentiousness frightened me off* . . .

And also—I must add this further admission, which is more serious —because I felt a certain contempt for her, from a social point of view. I considered her a "tramp" (which she was, as a matter of fact) and would never have dared appear with her in any of the places I ordinarily frequented. This is why, with typical cowardice, I preferred the company of whores, even more licentious but more amusing, who paid no attention to me.

Page 141, line 35: . . . *I manage to understand somewhat better* . . .

Today, I would no longer explain this in psychoanalytic terms and by invoking castration. Instead of a punishment both feared and desired, I would refer to my fear of committing myself, of assuming responsibilities—whence my tendency, counterbalanced by an inverse desire, to evade any virile determination—a general attitude I adopted with regard to life (which can only be lived on condition that one accepts death) and an attitude of which what I feel about physical love is no more than a particular case.

Page 142, line 18: . . . *of ignominy and, still more, of terror* . . .

I should have written "shame" and "anguish" rather than "ignominy" and "terror." For these words still relate to an act I am putting on for myself, whereas things that are strictly ignominious or terrible, far from being exciting for me, have always tended to make me draw back into my shell.

Page 144, line 19: . . . *in a long white nightgown* . . .

In this dream, the woman who appears in a long white nightgown seems to be essentially my *witness*, in other words: the eyes that observe the unrolling of my life, before whom my life must assume some meaning and by whom I shall be judged as deserving or guilty. But in what links me to her there is something more tender and more ambiguous than this relation of a moral order.

One may not have forgotten an important date in childhood, the first time one tastes certain dishes which are regarded as precious. Thus for me, the sinister day when I was given sherbet; for her, the revelation of bananas when, as a little girl, she had been taken to have a tooth pulled in the town nearest her home; in order to console her for the pain she had suffered, the person who had taken her had bought one of these beautiful fruits now so common but rare at the time, not so many years ago, outside Paris. My heart breaks at the thought of this present, supposedly a compensation, to the child who has become my lifetime companion: how poignant these consolations offered to children in order to make them forget into what a trap, coming into the world, they have fallen.

On the same emotional plane, though oriented somewhat toward the illicit: Sade's Justine who, still a child, masturbates in bed at night, on the advice of her older sister who has just left the convent, when she suffers too cruelly from the recent death of her father; the young bride (Janet Gaynor's role in Murnau's *Sunrise*) whose husband (George O'Brien, star of so many films of ruin and resurrection) offered her a piece of cake at a village fair because he had been tempted to drown her in order to pursue a whore he had just seen.

In 1964, these notes of some twenty years ago should be completed by many others. I shall include at least this one.

Page 89, line 7: . . . *that other piece of rubbish by Puccini* . . .

Since March 19th, 1951, when I attended a performance of that musical Western *The Girl of the Golden West* at the San Carlo in Naples, I have had a real passion for Puccini's music. Corrupt, certainly, but not vulgar, consistently adequate to the fluctuations of the drama, ardent, light and at times extremely vehement without ever breaking the marvellous flow, it certainly belongs to the lineage engendered by Monteverdi. For that friend of Tasso not only oriented the nascent opera towards realism and made it accessible to a wider public than that of the court, but was guided by a literally 'expressionistic' concern: to create a music that would emphasize language and its emotive charge.

The development of a throat cancer prevented Puccini from completing *Turandot*, that sumptuous *chinoiserie* which, forsaking *verismo* for Gozzi, tells the story of a princess who has her suitors beheaded when they fail to solve her riddles. Against this cousin of the Sphinx and of Judith stands, like another Lucrece, a touching figure devised by the librettists to the composer's specifications: the young slave-girl Liu, who stabs herself to preserve the victorious suitor's incognito, knowing he will die if she reveals his name. The musician who had already been inspired by Butterfly's *hara-kiri* survived this other suicide only briefly, and Liu's death-scene is the last he wrote. 'The opera will be performed incomplete, and someone will come on stage to say: "At this point, the Maestro laid down his pen",' is what Puccini is supposed to have said while he was composing the work which he intended to conclude with his finest love-duet and which he hoped to endow with all the weighty significance of a testament. Already tormented by disease, this popular composer had not hesitated to drive over seventy miles to satisfy his burning curiosity about the work of a musician still rejected by almost everyone but mentioned by some as a great innovator: Arnold Schönberg, with whom, at the concert's end, he enjoyed a friendly chat.

In 1958, when I visited Torre del Lago, Puccini's villa which has been transformed into a museum, I was shown the upright piano at which he worked, and I was told, before being led to the private chapel where he is buried, that the grave is located just behind the wall against which the instrument stands. I could not help thinking that it was this ebony piece of furniture which the artist had chosen for his coffin, as if, by entrusting his remains to the piano which his music had but lately animated and which represented the womb in which his hold on the present had been formed, he spectacularly asserted that the dead can lead, under the cloak of art, a second life. A fortune comparable to that of the Unknown Prince who, in *Turandot*, manages to transform into a tender beloved the icy princess at whose hands he seemed likely to suffer only the bloody fate of a Jokanaan or a Holofernes.

AFTERWORD
The Autobiographer
as *Torero*

"Accordingto the boundary that French law traces across the lifetime of every man under its jurisdiction—to which his birth has made him subject—it was in 1922 that the author of *Manhood* reached the climacteric which inspired the title of his book. In 1922: four years after the war which, like so many other boys of his generation, he had experienced as scarcely more than a long vacation, as one of them called it.

"In 1922, the author entertained few illusions as to the reality of the link that, theoretically, united an actual maturity with his legal majority. By 1935, when he completed his book, he no doubt supposed his existence had already sustained enough vicissitudes for him to pride himself on having attained the age of virility at last. Now in 1939, when the young men of the post-war period see the utter collapse of that structure of facility which they despaired of trying to invest with not only an authentic fervor but a terrible distinction as well, the author freely acknowledges that his true "manhood" still remains to be written, when he will have suffered, in one form or another, the same bitter ordeal his elders faced.

"However unjustified his book's title may appear today, the author has decided to retain it, convinced that, all things considered, it does not belie his ultimate intent: the search for a vital fulfillment that cannot be realized without a *catharsis*, a liquidation for which literary activity—and particularly the so-called literature of confession—appears to be one of the most suitable instruments.

"Among the many autobiographical novels, private journals, memoirs, and confessions that in recent years have enjoyed so extraordinary a vogue (as if the *creative* aspect of a literary work were subordinate to the problem of *expression,* the object produced merely accessory to the man who conceals—or parades—himself behind it), *Manhood* is therefore offered without any claim on its author's part to more than having tried to talk about himself with the maximum of lucidity and sincerity.

"One problem troubled his conscience and kept him from writing: is not what occurs in the domain of style valueless if it remains "aesthetic," anodyne, insignificant, if there is nothing in the fact of writing a work that is equivalent (and here supervenes one of the images closest to the author's heart) to the bull's keen horn, which alone—by reason of the physical danger it represents—affords the *torero*'s art a human reality, prevents it from being no more than the vain grace of a ballerina?

"To expose certain obsessions of an emotional or sexual nature, to admit publicly to certain shameful deficiencies or dismays was, for the author, the means—crude, no doubt, but which he entrusts to others, hoping to see it improved—of introducing even the shadow of a bull's horn into a literary work."

THIS was the preface I was writing for *Manhood* on the eve of the "phony war." I am rereading it today in Le Havre, a city I have so often visited for a few days' vacation and to which I am bound by many old ties (my friends Limbour, Queneau, and Salacrou, who were born here; Sartre, who taught here and with whom I became associated in 1941 when most of the writers remaining in occupied France united against the Nazi oppression). Le Havre is now largely destroyed, as I can see from my balcony, which overlooks the harbor from a sufficient height and distance to give a true picture of the terrible *tabula rasa* the bombs made in the center of the city, as if there has been an

attempt to repeat in the real world, on a terrain populated by
living beings, the famous Cartesian operation. On this scale, the
personal problems with which *Manhood* is concerned are obviously insignificant: whatever might have been, in the best of
cases, its strength and its sincerity, the poet's inner agony,
weighed against the horrors of war, counts for no more than a
toothache over which it would be graceless to groan; what is the
use, in the world's excruciating uproar, of this faint moan over
such narrowly limited and individual problems?

Yet even in Le Havre, things continue, urban life persists.
Above the still intact houses as above the site of the ruins there
shines intermittently, despite the rainy weather, a bright, beautiful sun. Boat basins and gleaming roofs, a whitecapped sea in the
distance, and the gigantic wasteland of the razed neighborhoods
(long since abandoned, as for some astounding "crop rotation")
submit—when the climate allows—to the influence of the aerial
humidity perforated by the sun's rays. Motors hum; trolleys and
bicycles pass; people stroll by or are busy at work; and many
chimneys send up their columns of smoke. I contemplate all this,
a spectator who has not taken the plunge (or who has only dipped
in his toe) and who shamelessly claims the right to admire this
half-devastated landscape as he might a beautiful painting, gaug-
ing in light and shade, in pathetic nakedness and picturesque
bustle, the place still inhabited today where a tragedy, hardly
more than a year ago, was enacted.

I WAS dreaming, then, of a bull's horn. I found it hard to resign
myself to being nothing more than a *littérateur*. The matador
who transforms danger into an occasion to be more brilliant
than ever and reveals the whole quality of his style just when he
is most threatened: that is what enthralled me, that is what I
wanted to be. By means of an autobiography dealing with a
realm in which discretion is *de rigueur*—a confession whose
publication would be dangerous to the degree that it would be
compromising and likely to make more difficult, by making more

explicit, my private life—I intended to rid myself for good of
certain agonizing images, at the same time that I revealed my
features with the maximum of clarity and as much for my own
use as to dissipate any erroneous sense of myself which others
might have. To effect a *catharsis,* to achieve my definitive liberation, this autobiography would have to take the form most
capable of rousing my own enthusiasm and of being understood
by other people as well. For this I counted on the strictest care
taken in the actual writing and on the tragic light shed on the
whole of my narrative by the very symbols I would employ:
Biblical and classical figures, heroes of the stage or else the
torero—psychological myths which affected me by their revela-
tory power and constituted, for the literary aspect of the operation, not only motifs but intermediaries suggesting an apparent
greatness where I knew only too well there was no such thing.

   To paint the clearest and closest portrait of the person I was
(as some artists brilliantly render sordid landscapes or everyday
utensils), to let artistic preoccupations intervene only with regard to style and composition: this is what I undertook to do, as
if I had anticipated that my talent as a painter and whatever
exemplary lucidity I might manifest would compensate for my
mediocrity as a model, and as if, in particular, an extension of
the moral order would result for me from the difficulties of such
an undertaking, since—even without eliminating some of my
weaknesses—I should at least have proved myself capable of that
objective gaze turned upon myself.

   What I did not realize was that at the source of all introspec-
tion is a predilection for self-contemplation, and that every confession contains a desire to be absolved. To consider myself ob-
jectively was still to consider myself—to keep my eyes fixed on
myself instead of turning them beyond and transcending myself
in the direction of something more broadly human. To expose
myself to others, but to do so in a narrative which I hoped would
be well-written and well-constructed, perceptive and moving
was an attempt to seduce my public into being indulgent, to

limit—in any case—the scandal by giving it an aesthetic form.
I believe, then, that if there has been a risk, a bull's horn, it is
not without a certain duplicity that I have ventured to accept
it: yielding, on the one hand, once again to my narcissistic tendency; trying, on the other, to find in my neighbor less a judge
than an accomplice. Similarly, the matador who seems to risk
everything is concerned about his "line" and relies, in order to
overcome the danger, on his technical sagacity.

Still, for the *torero* there is a real danger of death, which never
exists for the artist except outside his art (for instance, during
the German occupation, there was a clandestine literature which
involved genuine danger, but insofar as it was part of a much
more general struggle and, after all, independent of the writing
itself). Am I therefore justified in maintaining the comparison
and in regarding as valid my attempt to introduce "even the
shadow of a bull's horn into a literary work"? Can the fact of
writing ever involve, for the man who makes it his profession, a
danger which if not mortal is at least positive?

To write a book that is an act—such is, broadly, the goal that
seemed to be the one I must pursue when I wrote *Manhood*. An
act in relation to myself, since I meant, in writing it, to elucidate
by this very formulation certain still obscure things to which my
psychoanalysis, without making them entirely clear, had drawn
my attention. An act in relation to others, since it was apparent
that despite my oratorical precautions, the way in which I would
be regarded by others would no longer be what it had been before publication of this confession. An act, finally, on the literary
level, consisting of a backstage revelation that would expose, in
all their unenthralling nakedness, the realities which formed the
more or less disguised warp, beneath surfaces I had tried to make
alluring, of my other writings. This was less a matter of what is
known as *littérature engagée* than of a literature in which I
was trying to engage myself completely. Within as without: expecting it to change me, to enlarge my consciousness, and to introduce, too, a new element into my relations with other people,

beginning with my relations with those close to me, who could no longer be quite the same once I had exposed what may have been already suspected, but only in a vague and uncertain way. This was no desire for a brutal cynicism, but actually a longing to confess everything in order to be able to start afresh, maintaining with those whose affection or respect I valued relations henceforth without dissimulation.

From the strictly aesthetic point of view, it was a question of condensing, in the almost raw state, a group of facts and images which I refused to exploit by letting my imagination work upon them; in other words: the negation of a novel. To reject all fable, to admit as materials only actual facts (and not only probable facts, as in the classical novel), nothing but these facts and all these facts, was the rule I had imposed upon myself. Already a trail had been blazed for me in this direction by André Breton's *Nadja*, but I dreamed above all of making my own that project Baudelaire was inspired to undertake after reading a passage in Poe's *Marginalia:* to lay bare one's heart, to write that book about oneself in which the concern for sincerity would be carried to such lengths that, under the author's sentences, "the paper would shrivel and flare at each touch of his fiery pen."

For various reasons—divergences of ideas, as well as personal differences it would take too long to discuss here—I had broken with surrealism. Yet it was nonetheless true that I remained steeped in it. Receptivity to what appears to be *given* without our having sought it (automatic writing, *objet trouvé*); poetic value attached to dreams (considered also as rich in insight); broad faith in Freudian psychology (which has mined an alluring ore of images and moreover affords every man a convenient means of achieving the tragic level by seeing himself as a new Oedipus); repugnance for everything that is a transposition or arrangement, in other words a fallacious compromise between real facts and the pure products of the imagination; insistence on speaking frankly (particularly about love, which bourgeois hypocrisy all too readily treats as the subject for entertainment

when it does not relegate it to the domain of the forbidden):
these are some of the great lines of force—encumbered by much
dross and not without some contradictions—that continued to
pass through me when I had the idea of this work in which are
confronted childhood memories, accounts of real events, dreams
and actually experienced impressions, in a kind of surrealist col-
lage or rather photomontage, since no element is utilized which
is not of strict veracity or of documentary value. This predilection for realism—not feigned, as in most novels, but positive
(since it was exclusively a matter of things experienced and presented without the least disguise)—was not only imposed upon
me by the nature of what I wanted to do (take my bearings and
publicly reveal myself), but also corresponded to an aesthetic
requirement: to speak only of what I knew from experience and
what touched me most closely, so that each of my sentences
would possess a special density, an affecting plenitude; in other
words: the quality proper to what we call "authenticity." To tell
the truth, in order to achieve this resonance so difficult to define
and which the word "authentic" (applicable to such diverse
things, and among others to purely poetic creations) is a far cry
from having explained: that is what I was tending toward, my
conception of the art of writing here converging with my moral
notion of my "engagement" in writing.

Turning to the *torero*, I observe that for him, too, there is a
code which he cannot infringe and an authenticity, since the
tragedy he acts out is a real tragedy, one in which he sheds blood
and risks his own skin. The point is to discover if, under such
conditions, the relation I establish between his authenticity
and my own is not based on a mere play on words.

Let us grant once and for all that to write and publish an
autobiography does not involve, for the man who undertakes
such a thing (unless he has committed an offense whose admission makes him liable to capital punishment) any danger of
death, except under exceptional circumstances. Undoubtedly he
risks suffering in his relations with those close to him, and risks

social opprobrium if his avowals run too counter to accepted ideas; but it is possible, even if he is not a pure cynic, that such punishments may be of little enough consequence for him (may even please him, should he regard as salubrious the atmosphere thus created around him), so that he is dealing with an entirely fictional risk. Whatever the case, a moral risk of this kind cannot be compared with the bodily risk the *torero* faces. Even conceding a common measure between them on the level of *quantity* (if the attachment of some people and the opinions of others count as much or more for me than my life itself, though in this realm it is easy to be mistaken), the danger to which I expose myself by publishing my confession differs radically, on the level of *quality,* from that which the matador constantly assumes in performing his role. Similarly, what may be aggressive in one's intention of proclaiming the truth about oneself (since those one loves might suffer thereby) remains quite different from a killing, whatever the havoc one provokes. Should I therefore regard as misleading the analogy I had sketched between two spectacular means of acting and of incurring danger?

I have already spoken of the fundamental rule (to tell the whole truth and nothing but the truth) to which the writer of confessions is bound, and I have also alluded to the precise ceremony to which, in his combat, the *torero* must conform. For the latter, it is evident that the code, far from being a protection, contributes to his danger: to deliver the thrust under the requisite conditions demands, for instance, that he put his body, during an appreciable length of time, within reach of the horns; hence there is an immediate connection between obedience to the rule and the danger incurred. Now, all things considered, is it not to a danger directly proportional to the rigor of the rule he has imposed on himself that the confessional writer is exposed? For to tell the whole truth and nothing but the truth is not all: he must also confront it directly and tell it without artifice, without those great arias intended to make it acceptable, tremolos or catches in the voice, grace notes and gildings which would have no other result than to disguise it to whatever degree, even by merely attenutating its crudity, by making less noticeable what might be shocking about it. This fact that the danger incurred depends on a more or less close observance of the rule therefore represents what I can, without too much presumption, retain of the comparison I chose to establish between my activity as a writer of confessions and that of the *torero*.

If it seemed to me, originally, that to set down an account of my life from an erotic point of view (a preferential one, since sexuality then seemed to me the cornerstone in the structure of the personality), if it seemed to me that a confession bearing on what Christianity calls "the works of the flesh" was enough to make me, by the act this represents, a kind of *torero*, I must still consider whether the rule I had imposed upon myself—a rule whose rigor, I was satisfied to note, endangered me—is actually comparable, relation to danger aside, to that which dictates the *torero*'s movements.

In a general way, one might say that the bullfighting code pursues one essential goal: aside from the fact that it obliges a man to incur serious danger (while arming him with an indispensable technique), and not to dispatch his adversary just anyhow, it prevents the combat from being a mere slaughter; as punctilious as a ritual, it presents a tactical aspect (put the bull in a state to receive the final thrust though without having exhausted the animal more than was necessary), but also an aesthetic aspect: to the degree that the man is "exposed in profile," as he must be when giving his sword thrust, there is an arrogance in his posture; to the degree that his feet remain motionless throughout a series of close and fluid passes, the cape moving slowly, he forms with the beast that glamorous amalgamation in which man, material, and the huge horned mass seem united by a play of reciprocal influences; everything combines, in a word, to imprint upon the confrontation of bull and *torero* a *sculptural* character.

Looking on my enterprise as a sort of photomontage and

choosing for my expression a tone as objective as possible, trying to gather my life into a single solid block (an object I can
touch, as though to insure myself against death, even when,
paradoxically, I am claiming to risk everything), even if I opened
my door to dreams (a psychologically justified element but
tinged with romanticism, just as the *torero*'s cape work, technically useful, is also a series of lyrical flights), I was imposing on
myself a rule quite as severe as if I had intended to compose a
classical work. And it is ultimately this very severity, this "clas-
sicism"—not excluding such excess as one finds in even our most
formalized tragedies and relying not only on considerations of
form but on the notion of thereby achieving a maximum of
veracity—which seems to me to have afforded my undertaking
(if I have managed to succeed at all) something analogous to
what constitutes for me the exemplary value of the *corrida* and
which the imaginary bull's horn could not have contributed by
itself.

To use materials of which I was not the master and which I
had to take as I found them (since my life was what it was and
I could not alter, by so much as a comma, my past, a primary
datum representing for me a fate as unchallengeable as for the
torero the beast that runs into the ring), to say everything and
say it without "doctoring," without leaving anything to the
imagination and as though obeying a necessity—such was the
risk I accepted and the law I had fixed for myself, such the ceremony with which I could make no compromise. Though the
desire to *expose myself* (in every sense of the term) has constituted the first impulse, the fact remained that this *necessary*
condition was not a *sufficient* condition, and that, further, it
was from this original goal that the form to be adopted had to
be deduced, with the almost automatic force of an obligation.
These images I gathered together, this tone I employed—at the
same time that they deepened and sharpened my self-awareness
—had to be (unless I failed) what would accord my emotion a
better chance of being shared. Similarly, the order of the *corrida*
(a rigid framework imposed on an action in which, theatrically,

chance must appear to be dominated) is a technique of combat and at the same time a ritual. It was therefore necessary that this method I had imposed upon myself—dictated by the desire to see into myself as clearly as possible—function simultaneously and effectively as a rule of composition. Identity, so to speak, of form and content, but, more precisely, a unique procedure revealing the content to me as I gave it form, a form that could be of interest to others and (at its extreme) allow them to discover in themselves something homophonous to this content I had discovered in myself.

Obviously I am formulating this quite *a posteriori,* in order to define as well as I can the procedure I used, and without being qualified, of course, to decide if this "tauromachic" code, a guide for action and a guarantee against complacency, has turned out to be capable of such effectiveness as a means of style, or even (as to certain details) if what I claimed to see as a necessity of method did not actually correspond to an ulterior motive concerning composition.

I distinguish in literature a genre of major significance to me, which would include those works where the horn is present in one form or another, where the author assumes the direct risk either of a confession or of a subversive work, a work in which the human condition is confronted directly or "taken by the horns" and which presents a conception of life "engaging" its partisan—or its victim; works showing an attitude of something like humor or madness toward things, and the intent to make oneself the mouthpiece of the great themes of human tragedy. I can suggest in any case—but no doubt this is battering down an open door?—that it is precisely to the degree that one cannot see in a work any other rule of composition than the Ariadne's thread the author followed throughout the explanation he was making (by successive approaches or at point-blank range) to himself that works of this genre can be regarded, in literary terms, as "authentic." This by definition, from the moment one admits that literary activity, in its specific aspect as a mental discipline, cannot have any other justification than to *illuminate*

*certain matters for oneself at the same time as one makes them
communicable to others,* and that one of the highest goals that
can be assigned to literature's pure form, by which I mean
poetry, is to restore by means of words certain intense states,
concretely experienced and become significant, to be thus put
into words.

AT THIS point I am far from utterly immediate and dismaying
events such as the destruction of a great part of Le Havre, so
different today from the city I knew, and despoiled of those
places to which, subjectively, I was attached by memories: the
Hôtel de l'Amirauté, for instance, and the hot streets with their
buildings now flattened or gutted, like the one on whose wall
still remains the inscription "La Lune The Moon," with a
drawing of a smiling face within the lunar disc. There is the
beach, too, strewn with a strange foliage of scrap iron and labori-
ously piled stones, facing the sea where the other day a freighter
was blown up by a mine, adding its wreck to so many others. I
am far, indeed, from that authentic horn of the war of which I
see, in the ruined houses, only the least sinister effects. Were
I more "engaged" physically, more active, and thereby more
threatened, perhaps I should consider the literary phenomenon
more lightly. Perhaps I should be less obsessed by my desire to
make literature into an *act,* a drama by which I insist on incurring, positively, a risk—as if this risk were the necessary condition for my self-realization as a whole man. There would nonetheless remain that essential "engagement" one has the right to
demand of the writer, the engagement that derives from the very
nature of his art: not to misuse the language and therefore to
make his words, however he is able to set them down on paper,
always tell the truth. And on the intellectual or emotional level,
he must contribute evidence to the trial of our present system of
values and tip the scales, with all the weight by which he is so
often burdened, toward the liberation of *all* men, without which
none can achieve his own.

SELECTED BIBLIOGRAPHY

A list of the principal works of Michel Leiris, with the dates of their first appearance

Anthropology

L'AFRIQUE FANTÔME (Gallimard, Paris, 1934)

LA LANGUE SECRÈTE DES DOGONS DE SAGNA (Institut d'Ethnologie, Paris, 1948)

RACE ET CIVILISATION (UNESCO, Paris, 1951), translated as RACE AND CULTURE (UNESCO, Paris, 1951)

CONTACTS DE CIVILISATIONS EN MARTINIQUE ET EN GUADELOUPE (collection RACE ET SOCIÉTÉ, UNESCO-Gallimard, Paris, 1955)

L'UNIVERS DES FORMES: L'AFRIQUE NOIRE (with Jacqueline Delange) (Gallimard, Paris, 1967)

Literature

SIMULACRE (Galerie Simon, Paris, 1925)

LE POINT CARDINAL (Sagittaire, Paris, 1927)

TAUROMACHIES (G. L. Mano, Paris, 1937)

MIROIR DE LA TAUROMACHIE (G. L. Mano, Paris, 1938)

GLOSSAIRE J'Y SERRE MES GLOSES (Galerie Simon, Paris, 1939–40)

L'ÂGE D'HOMME (Gallimard, Paris, 1939)

NUITS SANS NUITS (Fontaine, Paris, 1945)

AURORA (Gallimard, Paris, 1946)

ANDRÉ MASSON ET SON UNIVERS (with Georges Limbour) (Trois Collines, Geneva, 1947)

THE PRINTS OF JOAN MIRO (Curt Valentin, New York, 1947)

LA RÈGLE DU JEU, I: BIFFURES (Gallimard, 1948)

LA RÈGLE DU JEU, II: FOURBIS (Gallimard, 1955)

LA RÈGLE DU JEU, III: FIBRILLES (Gallimard, 1966)

LA RÈGLE DU JEU, IV: FRÊLE BRUIT (Gallimard 1968)

The Author

MICHEL LEIRIS was born in Paris in 1901. He was a member of the Surrealist group from 1924 to 1929. He served in Africa as a member of the Mission Dakar-Djibouti from 1931–1933. He returned to Africa in 1945 to pursue his professional interests as an anthropologist. He has traveled widely in the French Caribbean, Egypt, North Africa (where he was a soldier in 1939) and China.

He has written critical studies of Raymond Roussel, Picasso, André Masson, Joan Miro, and Albert Giacometti. He has meditated at length on the art of bullfighting in several books, as well as in the commentary to Pierre Braunberger's film, *La Course de Taureaux*.

As a poet, his Surrealist works of the Thirties and Forties are appreciated. His greatest effort as a writer, however, has been devoted to anthropology and to a major autobiographical enterprise that opens, in 1939, with *L'Âge d'Homme* (MANHOOD) and continues with the four parts of *La Règle du Jeu: Biffures* (1948), *Fourbis* (1955), *Fibrilles* (1966), and *Frêle Bruit* (1968).